JOURNEY THROUGH

ANCIENT
CIVILIZATIONS

JOURNEY THROUGH

ANCIENT
CIVILIZATIONS

ROGER COOTE

SMITHMARK

First published in the United States in 1992 by
SMITHMARK Publishers Inc., 16 East 32nd Street,
New York, NY 10016

Copyright © 1992 Reed International Books Ltd.

ISBN 0-8317-5227-0

Printed in Italy

SMITHMARK books are available for bulk purchase for sales promo-
tion and premium use. For details write or telephone the manager of
Special Sales, SMITHMARK Publishers Inc., 16 East 32nd Street,
New York, NY 10016. (212) 532-6600

CONTENTS

THE FIRST HUMANS

Around 10 million years ago, the climate in Africa was changing, and areas of thick forest were being replaced by grasslands. The apes that lived in the forest trees began spending more of their time on the ground, searching for plants to eat. Gradually they learned to stand and walk on two legs, which meant they could use their hands for other things, including gathering food.

Over millions of years, the apes evolved into what are called hominids - human-like creatures. The earliest hominids, now known as australopithecines, appeared around 4 million years ago in East and southern Africa. Archaeologists have found fossil footprints, preserved in hardened volcanic ash, which show that australopithecines walked upright. They have also discovered parts of the skeleton of a female, nicknamed Lucy, who lived 3.4 million years ago in what is now Ethiopia.

Toolmakers

There were four different species of australopithecines. By about 2 million years ago, one species had developed into a creature called *Homo*, which had a larger brain than its ancestors and a more human-looking face. The earliest *Homo* species differed from the australopithecines in another, important way: it could make tools such as axes and scrapers by chipping flakes from stones to make a sharp edge. For this reason it has been christened *Homo habilis*, or "handy man."

The *Homo habilis* species may have used their tools for hunting animals, but it is more likely that they used them simply for cutting and scraping meat from carcasses that they found. Their major source of food was still plants, nuts, and berries. It is thought that they built small huts to shelter in - the first buildings in the world.

Hunter–Gatherers and Modern Humans

Around 1.7 million years ago, *Homo habilis* evolved into *Homo erectus*, the first hominid to hunt animals for food. At first they killed small creatures, such as bushpigs and hares, but as they learned to hunt in groups they tackled larger prey, including giant baboons. Meat was not their only food: they also ate various different types of plant, including roots that they dug from the earth.

The *Homo erectus* species were the first people to venture from Africa to Europe and Asia. As they moved northward, they had to adapt to living in the colder climates they found. This was possible partly because they had discovered how to make fire by rubbing sticks together, and therefore could keep warm. Fire also enabled them to cook meat and keep dangerous wild animals away.

A new species, *Homo sapiens neanderthalensis*, which was very like modern humans, evolved from *Homo erectus* between 200,000 and 150,000 years ago. Groups of Neanderthals, as they are known, lived in Europe, parts of the Middle East, and what was until recently southern U.S.S.R. Although they are often thought of as primitive cave men, they were much more intelligent than their ancestors and could make better tools. They also appear to have looked after old and sick members of their group, even though these people would not have been able to take part in hunting. Some Neanderthals lived in huts built from animal skins and the bones of mammoths - huge elephantlike creatures that were hunted for food.

Truly modern humans, *Homo sapiens sapiens*, first appeared in Africa about 100,000 years ago. They moved on into Europe and replaced other human species, including the Neanderthals, around 35,000 years ago. Modern humans also reached Australia from Asia 50,000 years ago and North America from Asia about 40,000 years ago.

Below: A Neanderthal hut made from mammoth bones and skins.

Below: By hunting in groups and using clubs as weapons, *Homo erectus* was able to kill large animals such as baboons.

THE DEVELOPMENT OF MODERN HUMANS

Our evolution from hominids (australopithecines) to modern humans (*Homo sapiens*) took 4 million years. Each new creature that evolved had a larger brain than the one before.

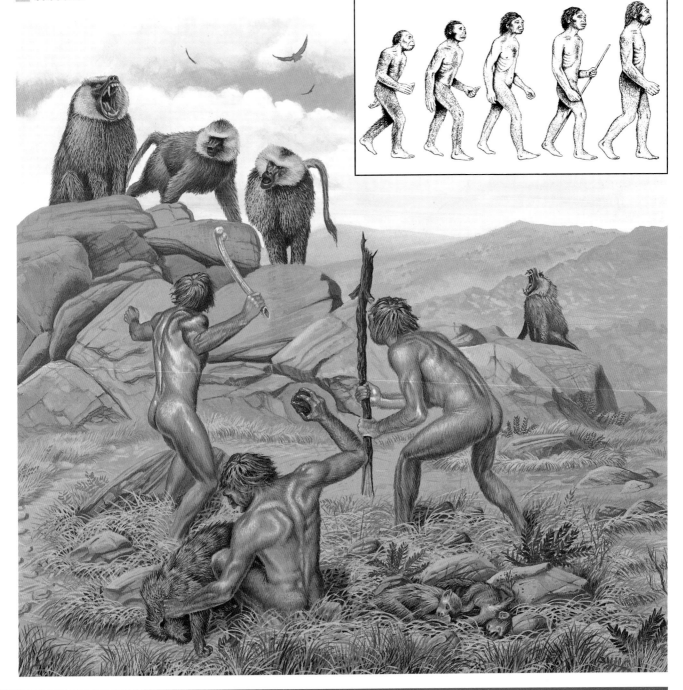

THE FIRST FARMERS

Around 12,000 years ago, important changes began to happen in an area known as the Fertile Crescent - what we now call Turkey, Israel, Iraq, and Iran. The climate was becoming warmer and more moist, and this helped wild plants - especially grasses - to grow in abundance. The hunter-gatherers who lived there discovered that the seeds of these grasses were good to eat, and they began harvesting them with flint-bladed knives. Gradually, they learned to produce more food by planting the grass seeds themselves. They planted the best seeds they could find and the crops slowly improved until they became like

Below: The farming village of Çatal Hüyük covered an area of 33 acres.

Right: The Fertile Crescent, where agriculture first began about 12,000 years ago.

FARMING BEGINS c.12,000 YEARS AGO • FIRST SETTLEMENTS 9,500 YEARS AGO

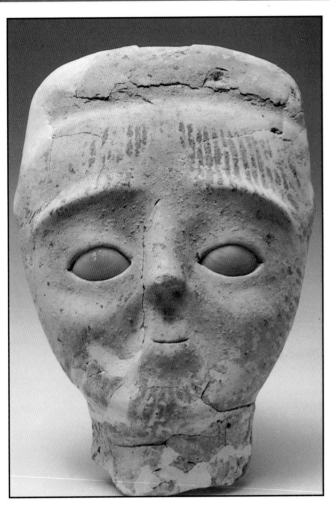

Above: This statue was made in Jericho over 8,000 years ago. The eyes are made from shells.

the cereals we know today - barley, wheat, and rye. These first farmers also started to keep animals, such as sheep and goats, for meat and milk.

People in other places were learning how to farm, too. Yams were grown in Southeast Asia around 9,000 years ago, and cereal crops were first cultivated in China and Central America more than 7,000 years ago.

The hunter-gatherers of the past had moved from place to place, searching for new supplies of food. When people began farming they were able to settle in one place, and this meant they could build permanent homes to live in. The farmers made their homes close together and built walls around their settlements to protect themselves from attackers. These were the first settled communities in the world.

Jericho

Around 9,500 years ago, a group of farmers settled at a site called Jericho in the Fertile Crescent. With its rich soil and a spring to provide water, the area was ideal for growing wheat and barley and for keeping sheep and goats. The farmers built huts for themselves using bricks made from dried mud, and constructed a strong stone wall, 10 ft. thick and 13 ft. high, around the settlement.

As more and more food was grown, the number of people who could be fed increased and the community grew. At one stage Jericho may have been home to as many as 2,000 people. Being able to grow more food also meant that not everyone had to work in the fields. Some people became specialized craftsmen, making tools, jewelry, and clay pots to store and cook food in.

Çatal Hüyük

The village of Çatal Hüyük, in what is now Turkey, was founded around 7,000 years ago. Like Jericho, it was surrounded by good farmland and it grew rapidly in size. The inhabitants became very wealthy by trading with other settlements. Nearby was a source of obsidian, a type of natural glass found in volcanic rocks that was used for making tools and ornaments. This was exchanged for other goods such as timber, copper, and even cowrie shells from as far away as the Red Sea. The craftsmen of Çatal Hüyük became very skilled at making copper jewelry, textiles, obsidian arrowheads and daggers, and carved stone figures. They also found out how to make bronze - a mixture of copper and tin - and tools made from bronze gradually replaced stone ones.

The people of Jericho had probably worshiped their ancestors. In Çatal Hüyük, religion became an increasingly important part of life. We do not know exactly what people believed in, although they may have worshiped bulls in especially built shrines. We do know that a group of priests and priestesses developed and became very powerful there.

BRONZE REPLACES STONE IN TOOLMAKING • RELIGION BECOMES MORE IMPORTANT

THE SUMERIANS

The first great civilization in the world, that of Sumer, developed in an area known as Mesopotamia around the Tigris and Euphrates rivers, in what is now Iraq. These two rivers, flowing through a dry, barren plain, played a vital part in the growth of Sumer: they provided water for agriculture and were used to transport goods for trade.

Sumerian farmers built complex systems of irrigation canals to carry water from the rivers to their fields. This enabled them to grow large amounts of barley, sesame, and onions. They also kept sheep, goats, pigs, and cattle. As more food was produced, the populations in some areas grew quickly, and by 3500 B.C. the world's first cities had appeared. Each city ruled over the land around it, and the whole of Mesopotamia consisted of city-states that often fought among themselves to gain more territory.

The Sumerians were so successful at producing food that many people did not have to work in the fields. Instead, they made pottery, textiles, and expensive luxuries, including fine clothes and ornaments, for wealthy inhabitants.

Trade, Religion, and Writing

Trade was important to the city-states. Mesopotamia could not produce all of the raw materials that the Sumerians needed, and hard stone and metals had to be brought in by boat from elsewhere. Gold, copper, timber, ivory, pearls, and precious stones were also imported from as far afield as Afghanistan, Persia, and India. The beautiful objects made by the manufacturers and craftsmen in the Sumerian cities were exported in return.

Keeping account of the large amount of goods moving in and out of a city was a complicated task. To make it simpler, clay counters were used. Later, the counters were kept in clay containers, called *bullas*, which were marked with symbols to show how many counters were inside. This was the first writing that had ever existed. The next step was the invention and use of more elaborate symbols to represent sheep, cows, and a variety of other goods, which eventually led to the development of a complete written language.

At first, the symbols of this new language closely resembled the objects they represented. Gradually, though, scribes began to write faster and found it easier to turn the symbols sideways. Eventually, the pictures developed into a type of wedge-shaped writing known as cuneiform. The writing was done by marking picture symbols on flat pieces of wet clay with the end of a reed stem. When the clay tablets dried, they became very hard and many have survived to the present day. The oldest ones to have been found date from 3100 B.C.

Ur

The city of Ur, in the south of Mesopotamia, became one of the greatest Sumerian states and ruled a large empire. By 2500 B.C. it was a major center of trade and manufacture, and 500 years later as many as 20,000 people may have lived there. The early rulers of Ur were extremely wealthy. They wore fine clothes and frequently held lavish banquets. When they died they were buried with fabulous ornaments made from costly materials, including gold and silver. The rulers' servants and attendants were sometimes sacrificed and buried with the rulers: one tomb held the bodies of 74 attendants.

BUILDING OF FIRST CITIES c.3500 B.C. • FIRST WRITTEN LANGUAGE 3100 B.C.

Above: When a Sumerian ruler died, his servants killed themselves and were buried with him.

Right: Part of the ruins of Ur on the banks of the Euphrates river.

In the center of the city, inside a sacred enclosure, was a building called a ziggurat. This was a massive three-storey temple dedicated to Nanna, the moon god. Outside the enclosure were other temples, palaces, two man-made harbors, and the houses of the city dwellers. The entire city was encircled by a wall made of hard, sun-baked mud bricks.

After about 1800 B.C., Ur began to lose its power and the land was taken over by a people called the Amorites. They established their own empire centered around the city of Babylon.

UR AT THE HEIGHT OF ITS POWER c.2500 -1800 B.C. • RISE OF THE AMORITES 1800 B.C.

ANCIENT EGYPT

Around 5000 B.C., farmers began to cultivate the rich soil which lay in a narrow strip on each side of the Nile River in Egypt and at the delta where the river flowed into the sea. This fertile soil was left behind after the river flooded each year. The land on each side was dry, barren desert, and without the Nile there would have been no early civilization in Egypt.

The population increased quickly and farming villages grew in size. The first walled cities appeared at Naqada and Hieraconopolis in about 3300 B.C., near the tombs of dead rulers. In 3100 B.C., Egypt became a unified state ruled by kings, called pharaohs, with its capital at Memphis.

The ancient Egyptians believed in life after death, and the tombs of kings and other rich people were filled with things that the dead person would need in the afterlife, including cooking pots and jewelry. Stone carvings and paintings decorated the walls. The body was buried in a pit and then covered with sand, which dried out the corpse and preserved it. It was believed that the person's spirit would then be able to recognize the body and return to it in the afterlife. A flat-topped structure, called a mastaba, was built over the pit using mud bricks.

The Pyramids

In about 2700 B.C., at the start of what is called the Old Kingdom, the Egyptians began to build a new type of tomb for their pharaohs. A stone pyramid was constructed at Saqqara, near Memphis, for the pharaoh Zoser. It had four sides that rose up in steps to a height of 203 ft. and was the largest structure the world had ever seen.

The Egyptians then began to prepare some bodies for the afterlife in a new way. When an important person died, his or her body was preserved by mummification. The person's insides were removed and the body was soaked in a special preserving fluid. It was then dried, wrapped in bandages, and buried inside several coffins in a deep tomb. Mummified bodies remained well preserved for many centuries.

Soon after this, even bigger pyramids were built, with smooth sides instead of steps. The Great Pyramid of King Khufu, built at Giza in about 2450 B.C., is 482 ft. high. It is thought to contain 2.3 million stone blocks, each weighing about 2½ tons. Around the

Above: This Egyptian hieroglyphic writing from Saqqara is about 4,500 years old.

Below: The Great Pyramid at Giza, where King Khufu was buried around 2450 B.C.

FIRST CITIES IN EGYPT c.3300 B.C. • BEGINNING OF THE OLD KINGDOM 2700 B.C.

12

huge pyramid are smaller ones built for Khufu's queens, mastabas for the bodies of the king's relatives and officials, and pits containing dismantled boats for use in the afterlife.

Work on building the pyramids and the "cities of the dead" that surrounded them was carried out from July to October each year. At that time, farmers could not cultivate their crops because the Nile was in flood and the fields were under water.

The End of the Old Kingdom

Ancient Egypt was governed by a group of ministers who were responsible to the king. The chief minister, or vizier, was in charge of administration, justice, and taxation. The country was divided into provinces, each ruled by a governor. By 2400 B.C., these governors had become extremely powerful and the pharaoh was unable to control them. The governers built up their own armies and raised taxes for themselves rather than for the pharaoh. But the final blow

to the Old Kingdom was caused by the very thing upon which life in Egypt depended - the Nile.

The annual flooding of the river was never very predictable, and in some years the water did not rise high enough to cover all the fields. Around 2150 B.C., there were several years of very low flooding. This greatly reduced the amount of food that could be grown and caused terrible famines, which destroyed the power of the kingdom.

Below: Egypt during the Old Kingdom, which began in 2700 B.C.

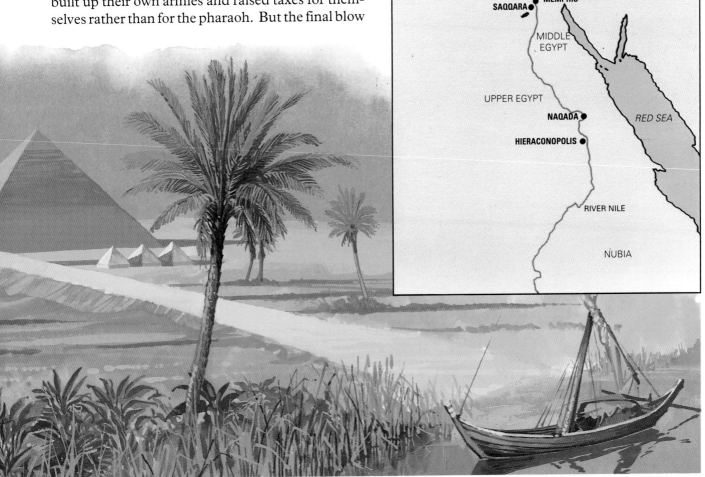

GREAT PYRAMID OF KHUFU FINISHED 2450 B.C. • OLD KINGDOM COLLAPSES 2150 B.C.

13

THE INDUS VALLEY

As had happened both in Egypt and Mesopotamia, the first great civilization in India grew up around a river - the Indus. The first cities developed around 2500 B.C. on a broad plain in the northwest of the subcontinent, with the Thar Desert on one side and the highlands of Baluchistan on the other. Like the Nile, the Indus floods each year and when the floodwaters recede they leave behind a layer of fertile silt over a large area. The Indus Valley civilization was able to develop because of this rich soil, on which barley and wheat could be grown without irrigation.

About 100 Indus settlements have been found dating from between 2500 and 2000 B.C., and most of them were quite sizeable towns surrounded by defensive walls of baked brick. The cities of the Indus Valley were the first places in the world where iron was produced by heating the iron ore that is found in rocks, a process called smelting. A form of writing was also invented there at approximately the same time.

As well as supporting their populations by growing crops, the towns seem to have traded with each other and with other civilizations. Archaeologists have found Indus seals - used for securing bales of merchandise - at sites in Mesopotamia, and some Mesopotamian goods in the Indus city of Mohenjo-daro. Much of this trade went by sea, although there were also overland trade routes to Afghanistan and Persia. Goods were probably carried along these land routes in bullock carts, because clay models of

Left: The first towns and cities in India grew up along the fertile valley of the River Indus. The largest were Harappa and Mohenjo-daro.

Below: The walled citadel of an Indus Valley city was surrounded by houses and rich agricultural land.

FIRST CITIES IN INDUS VALLEY c.2500 B.C. • WHEAT AND BARLEY MAIN CROPS GROWN

Right: A seal used by merchants and a clay model of a bullock cart from Mohenjo-daro.

carts have been found in a number of Indus towns and cities. The goods that were exported included cotton cloth - the first of its kind in the world - pottery, bead necklaces, and skilfully crafted shells and metalwork.

Mohenjo-daro and Harappa

The two largest cities of the Indus Valley were Mohenjo-daro, near to the point where the Indus flowed into the Arabian Sea, and Harappa, which was further upstream on a tributary of the Indus called the Chenab River.

Each of these two cities covered an area of about 148 acres and may have housed 40,000 people. In the center of both cities was an artificial mound, called a citadel, on which religious and government buildings were constructed. There was also a large granary where grain was stored so that there was enough to last all through the year.

The citadel overlooked the surrounding streets and houses. The streets were carefully planned, with rows of houses crossing at right angles and a system of sewers and drains. The larger houses consisted of a number of rooms built around an open courtyard. Some houses had bathrooms and toilets. The courtyard often had a brick-lined shaft in the floor, which may have been a well or a place to store jars and vases. Stairs in the courtyard led to the upper storey of the house or to a flat roof. Poorer people lived in houses with only one room.

Sudden Collapse

The Indus Valley civilization was well organized. The weights made for weighing goods were the same everywhere, as was the writing that was used, and in Mohenjo-daro and other cities the buildings were all constructed from bricks of the same standard size. Yet, the civilization seems to have ended suddenly in about 1500 B.C. We do not know for certain why this happened. Mohenjo-daro probably declined when the Indus changed its course, which meant that the surrounding fields were not fertilized when it flooded and therefore did not produce enough crops. Other towns were attacked by invaders from the north. What we do know is that the great towns and cities of the Indus Valley crumbled and were replaced by small farming villages.

FIRST COTTON TEXTILES MADE • CIVILIZATION ENDS SUDDENLY c.1500 B.C.

15

SHANG CHINA

Left: The first great civilization in China - the Shang - began around the Yellow River.

Below: An oracle bone with Chinese writing carved on it.

Bottom: These workmen are building a rammed-earth wall to protect their city.

YELLOW RIVER
ANYANG
ZHENGZHOU
YELLOW SEA
RIVER YANGTZE
SOUTH CHINA SEA

The world's fourth great civilization - after Sumer, Egypt, and the Indus Valley - grew up in northeast China. From about 4000 B.C. there were farming communities around the Yellow River and the Yangtze River. At first the people lived in temporary settlements, and survived by hunting, fishing, and growing a few crops before moving onto another site. Later they built larger, permanent villages and spent more of their time on agriculture.

FARMING VILLAGES NEAR YELLOW RIVER c.4000 B.C. • SHANG DYNASTY c.1800 B.C.

The early Chinese farmers depended on the rivers for water to grow their crops of millet, cabbages, and plums. They also used them for transport. But the presence of the rivers had major disadvantages as well, especially the floods that occasionally covered vast areas and drowned thousands of people.

The First Dynasty

Between about 2500 and 1800 B.C., during what is called the Longshan period, walled towns were built and crafts such as metalworking and pottery making developed in China. Around 1800 B.C., China's first dynasty, or ruling family, appeared at the start of the major civilization which has been named after them - the Shang.

The center of Shang China was on the western edge of the North China Plain. This is the area in which the Yellow River flows from the mountains to the north and drops its load of fertile silt. The fertile area extended east toward the Yellow Sea and south toward the Yangtze River. The main crop grown on the plain was millet, although in the east, rice was cultivated in paddy fields watered by the river. The northern mountains provided rich supplies of metals, including copper, tin, and gold. Shang craftsmen made weapons and beautiful ceremonial vases from bronze, and they were also skilled at painting with lacquer and carving stone and jade.

One of the earliest Shang capitals was at Zhengzhou, near the south of the fertile plain. It was founded in about 1700 B.C. At its center was a raised platform of earth, more than $5^{1}/_{2}$ mi. long and over $32^{1}/_{2}$ ft. high, which was surrounded by a wall. On the platform were the palace buildings of the ruling family, and outside the city walls were workshops and the houses where the ordinary citizens lived.

The Shang seem to have moved their capital city several times, possibly because of flooding or invasions by enemies. About 1400 B.C. Anyang became the capital. Around this city are graves, some of which are thought to contain the last of the Shang kings. Although these graves were robbed centuries ago, some of the items that remain - including bronze objects, jade and bone carvings, and cowrie shells that were used as money - suggest that they once contained treasures of immense value.

Religion and Warfare

Religion played an important role in Shang China. People worshiped their ancestors in their own homes and asked for their guidance on future events. They also heated bones - especially the shoulder blades of cattle - to make them crack, and then "read" the shapes of the cracks to tell fortunes. The earliest form of Chinese writing, dating from about 1400 B.C., was found carved on these so-called "oracle bones."

The Shang were always threatened by attackers from the north and west, and warfare was a central part of their society. War chariots and bronze weapons were sometimes buried with dead nobles. Eventually, the Shang dynasty came to an end during the eleventh century B.C., when nomads from the west invaded and established the Chou dynasty.

Below: A bronze vessel in the shape of a tiger protecting a man.

ZHENGZHOU BECOMES CAPITAL c.1700 B.C. • CHOU DYNASTY BEGINS c.1027 B.C.

17

IMPERIAL EGYPT

Above: Egypt at the time of the New Kingdom.

Egypt's Old Kingdom ended in about 2150 B.C. (see pages 12-13) and was followed by a period in which the country broke down into a network of provinces, each ruled by its own governor. In around 2040 B.C., Egypt's pharaohs managed to reunite the land and the era known as the Middle Kingdom began.

The Middle Kingdom

Life in the Middle Kingdom continued much as it had done in the days of the Old Kingdom. Agriculture was totally dependent upon the Nile. The river flooded every July to October, and crops were planted between November and February. Paintings inside tombs show farmers plowing their land, sowing crops, and harvesting wheat, barley, vegetables, lentils, and fruit. Despite the vital part farmers played in supplying Egypt with food, they were looked down upon by others. Priests, viziers, scribes, merchants, and craftsmen were all regarded as far superior to those who fed them.

The priests' duties involved serving in the temples which were built to honor Egypt's many gods and goddesses. Each *nome*, or administrative region, had its own god, and there were many others as well, including Ra, the sun god, Thoth, the moon god, Osiris, the god of the Underworld, and Anubis, the god of mummification. The pharaoh was thought to be a god himself - the living embodiment of the falcon-headed god Horus.

The viziers were very powerful because they were the pharaohs' advisers and supervised the royal court. Scribes also had the important job of overseeing the harvest and writing down how much of each crop had been produced. They also recorded the history of their times. Egyptian hieroglyphic writing was first used in about 3000 B.C., and at that time scribes wrote on clay tablets. About 400 years later, however, papyrus - a form of paper made from flattened reeds - was invented.

Craftsmen in cities and villages throughout Egypt produced beautiful metalwork, furniture, pottery, jewelry, and fabrics. These items were made both for use within Egypt and for export to other lands. The most skilful craftsmen were employed in the royal workshops, where they spent their time making furnishings for the pharaohs' tombs.

The New Kingdom

During the Middle Kingdom, the provinces once again started to become independent and power slipped away from the pharaohs around 1783 B.C. By 1570 B.C., they had regained their hold on the country and the New Kingdom began, with its center in the city of Thebes.

Between 1570 and 1080 B.C. Egypt reached the height of its wealth and power. Nubia, to the south, was seized, with its rich deposits of gold, and Syria and Palestine were also conquered. The craftsmen of the New Kingdom produced even finer work than before, as can be seen from the superb items found in the tomb of the pharaoh Tutankhamun.

When pharaohs died they were no longer buried in pyramids. Despite being carefully sealed to deter robbers, most pyramids had already been plundered of their treasures. The New Kingdom pharaohs decided to make their tombs less obvious by hiding them in a small valley across the river from Thebes - the Valley of the Kings. They were buried there,

MIDDLE KINGDOM c.2040-1783 B.C. • NEW KINGDOM 1570-1080 B.C.

Right and below: Treasures from Tutankhamun's grave in the Valley of the Kings.

with all the beautiful objects they would need in their life after death, in deep tombs cut out of the rock. Not even these precautions could protect them from the grave robbers, however, and only Tutankhamun's tomb remained undiscovered for long.

As had happened at the end of the Old Kingdom, there was a period in the twelfth century B.C. during which the flooding of the Nile became very unpredictable and famine swept through Egypt. The price of grain rose dramatically and riots broke out. To add to this, the country was attacked by land and sea during the reign of Rameses III (1198-1166 B.C.), the last great pharaoh. On land, the threat came from the Libyans to the west, on the sea from the "Sea Peoples," who came from various parts of the eastern Mediterranean. By 935 B.C., Egypt was ruled by kings from Libya.

Below: A funeral procession in the Valley of the Kings, across the Nile from the city of Thebes.

TUTANKHAMUN BURIED IN VALLEY OF KINGS 1337 B.C. • DEATH OF RAMESES III 1166 B.C.

PEOPLE OF THE STEPPES

The grasslands of The Steppes stretch right across Asia from Manchuria in the far north of China to the Ukraine in the southeast U.S.S.R. Although some parts of this vast area were inhabited between 5000 and 4000 B.C., others were too dry to be used for growing crops. After 2000 B.C., however, nomadic cultures grew up, and 1000 years later most of The Steppes were occupied.

Nomadic Life

There are very few remains of The Steppe civilizations. This is mainly because of their nomadic way of life, which involved moving constantly from place to place in search of new grazing land for their herds of cattle, sheep, and horses. These people never stopped for long in one area, so therefore they did not build permanent houses; instead they lived in tents which could be packed away and carried to the next site. Some permanent settlements were built, but these were mainly at the western edge of The Steppes near the Black Sea.

The most lasting evidence left by the nomads was in the form of burial mounds, called barrows. In some barrows, especially those of the Scythian people of southern Russia, rich treasures have been found, including gold weapons and jewelry, and silver vases for holding wine and oil. Some of the burial gifts made to dead Scythian chiefs were the work of local craftsmen, while others were produced by Greek artists. In the same way, Scythian art frequently showed local animals, including horses, yaks, lions, and wild boars, but other creatures not to be found in the surrounding area were also portrayed. We can, therefore, be sure that the Scythians came into contact with other civilizations.

Besides wearing jewelry, some nomadic people also decorated their bodies. The corpse of one chief, found at Pazyryk in Mongolia, had large tattoos on its skin. The people also changed the shape of their heads by binding babies' skulls tightly, forcing them to become extended as they grew.

Horse riding spread through The Steppes after 2000 B.C., and barrows often contain the skeletons of horses which were sacrificed when a chief died. Humans - probably the chief's servants - were also killed and buried with him in the barrow. Warfare

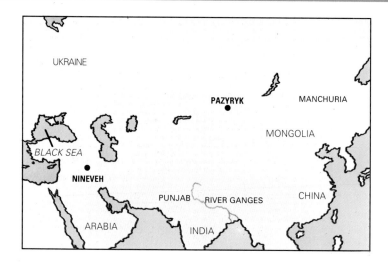

Above: Most of the vast area of The Steppes was occupied by 1000 B.C.

Below: Steppe nomads moving a herd of horses to new grazing land.

was common between the various nomadic groups; the warriors fought on horseback using bows, swords, and long lances.

Scythians in Mesopotamia and India

During the seventh century B.C., the Scythians began to play a part in the affairs of areas to the south of their lands. They occupied the mountains that formed the northern border of the Assyrian empire and then joined with the Medes and Babylonians to attack Assyria. They captured the Assyrians' cities one by one, and finally overran Nineveh, the capital, in 612 B.C. Later, the Persian empire led by Darius I attempted to conquer the Scythians. The nomads crushed Darius' army in battle on the plains of southern Russia, however, and he was forced back.

The Scythians remained unconquered until Philip of Macedon subdued them between 354 and 339 B.C. Even then Scythian power continued further east. One Scythian tribe moved down into India around 200 B.C. and occupied the Punjab and part of the Ganges River valley. It was later forced out and driven westward toward the Parthian empire. The Scythians caused the Parthians great problems and killed two of their kings in battle, but eventually they were absorbed into the Parthian empire.

Above: A wall hanging from a burial mound at Pazyryk showing a Steppe horseman.

WESTERN SCYTHIANS DEFEATED 354-339 B.C. • MOVE INTO INDIA c.200 B.C.

21

OCEANIA

The first people arrived in Australia between 70,000 and 50,000 years ago. They sailed across the sea from Southeast Asia and settled around the coasts of their new land. It must have been difficult for them to adapt, because they found plants and animals that were very different from those in their homeland.

Around 7,000 years ago, the level of the sea began to rise and the early Australians moved inland. They remained hunter-gatherers and fishermen, and did not discover how to grow crops or herd livestock until Europeans arrived in the eighteenth century A.D.

Melanesia

The small islands which make up Melanesia, to the northeast of Australia, were colonized much later than Australia itself. The first settlers sailed there from eastern Indonesia about 4,000 years ago, taking with them many of the things they needed to start a new life, including crop plants and animals. They also took their distinctive pottery, known as *Lapita*, which was very finely decorated.

The Melanesians were skilful boatbuilders; their sail-driven canoes had to be large and strong to carry themselves and their supplies on such a long voyage. The canoes' hulls were probably built from hollowed-out tree trunks. Each canoe consisted of two hulls, fixed beneath a row of curved timber supports. Passengers and cargo were carried on a platform which was tied on top of the supports. The largest canoes were more than 98 ft. long.

These early mariners must have been good navigators, too, as the tiny Melanesian islands are in the world's largest ocean, the Pacific. They steered their course by watching the positions of the stars and the Sun, and by studying the direction of the wind. They made navigation charts in the form of a framework of wooden strips on which cowrie shells were fixed to mark the position of islands (see top right). Some of the wooden strips showed places where there were strong ocean currents.

The Polynesian Islands

In about 1300 B.C., settlers reached the island of Fiji, at the eastern edge of Melanesia. Soon after, they sailed further east into what is called Polynesia. They arrived in Tonga and Samoa around 1100 B.C., and

Right: A Polynesian voyageur and a twin hulled canoe.

Below: Nearly all of Polynesia was settled by A.D. 1000.

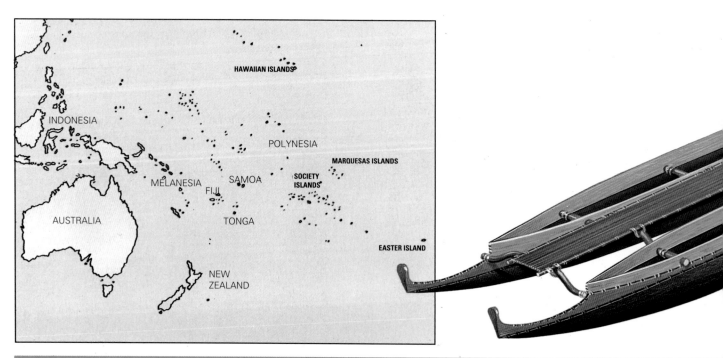

FIRST AUSTRALIANS 70,000-50,000 YEARS AGO • MELANESIA SETTLED c.2000 B.C.

22

remained there for more than 1,000 years, isolated from the rest of the world.

The people of Polynesia lived by fishing, growing crops such as yams, taro (a tropical plant with large, edible roots), coconuts, breadfruit, and bananas, and raising pigs and poultry. As well as their *Lapita* pottery, they made ornaments and tools from shells, obsidian, and stone.

In around 200 B.C., people from Samoa sailed their canoes to the east and settled in the Marquesas Islands. These islands became the center from which the rest of Polynesia was colonized. Canoes carrying settlers with their plants, animals, fishing equipment, and ornaments sailed from the Marquesas to the Hawaiian Islands in A.D. 400. By 800, Easter Island and the Society Islands had been colonized, and in around 900 people reached New Zealand.

By about A.D. 1000, almost every island in Polynesia had been visited and most of them had permanent settlements. Wherever the Polynesian people settled, they introduced new crops, animals, and farming methods. Their achievement is amazing because of the vast area in which their settlements are found; some of their sea voyages, made in open canoes, covered up to 2,400 miles.

Below: An early Aboriginal rock painting from Australia.

SETTLERS SPREAD FROM MARQUESAS THROUGHOUT POLYNESIA c.A.D. 300-1000

MINOAN CRETE

Left: This fresco showing leaping dolphins decorated the wall of the Queen's Room in the palace at Knossos.

Below: Minoans in the main courtyard at Knossos.
Inset: The palace.

START OF MINOAN CIVILIZATION c.2000 B.C. • GREAT PALACES BUILT 2000 TO 1700 B.C.

The Minoan civilization developed on the Mediterranean island of Crete, to the south of Greece. People first settled there in about 6000 B.C., and gradually small settlements and then larger towns appeared. According to legend, Crete was ruled by King Minos, who controlled the Aegean Sea with his powerful navy. We cannot be certain that Minos ever really existed, but he gave his name to Europe's first major civilization.

Between 2000 and 1700 B.C., a number of states grew up in Crete. They were established around the most important cities - Knossos, Phaistos, Mallia, and Zakro. These cities, which all had royal palaces at their center, were joined by a network of roads.

The Palace of Knossos

The largest and grandest of the Minoan palaces was at Knossos. The first palace there, built in 2000 B.C., was destroyed by an earthquake and then built once again in 1700 B.C. Ceremonial rooms and royal apartments were arranged around a central courtyard. The walls of the apartments were decorated with beautiful frescoes (made by painting onto wet plaster) showing fish and dolphins, court rituals, and sports. Beneath the apartments were storerooms filled with grains, wine, and olive oil. This produce was collected from the neighboring fields and redistributed to the people in the city and the nearby towns. The palace also had its own workshops,

where craftsmen worked gold, bronze, copper, gemstones, and ivory. Minoan potters were especially skilful, and produced finely decorated vases and pots for export to Egypt, Cyprus, and the Levant.

To one side of the palace was a second courtyard, which may have been used for spectator sports. One of the most popular sports was bull-leaping, which is depicted in many Minoan frescoes. The aim was to somersault over a bull as it charged, avoiding its long, sharp horns. In the frescoes, men are painted red and women white - a tradition that was used in Egypt at the same time.

Writing was another import from Egypt. Hieroglyphics were probably brought to Crete in around 1900 B.C., although the Minoans later developed their own style of writing, known as "Linear A." Examples of another script, "Linear B," have also been found in Crete, but it is probable that this was introduced by the Mycenaeans of mainland Greece (see pages 30-31). Writing was needed for keeping records of the goods passing into and out of palaces.

Minoan Gods

Unlike other civilizations at the time, the Minoans did not build temples to their gods. Instead, they worshiped in sacred caves in the mountains and in hilltop sanctuaries. They believed in a number of gods, although we do not know for certain who they were. The double-headed axe was a sacred emblem which probably symbolized a particular god; a gold axe dating from 1500 B.C. was found in the sacred cave at Arkalochri, southeast of Knossos. Minoan deities may have included a god of animals, a goddess of hunting, and a great Earth mother. Small shrines were built in ordinary homes, mostly to honor the snake goddess, who was regarded as the guardian spirit of the house.

The Minoan civilization came to a sudden end in about 1450 B.C. The reason may have been a huge volcanic eruption on the island of Thera, 78 mi. to the north, causing earthquakes and a tidal wave which destroyed the cities and their palaces. It is more likely, however, that the island, already weakened by natural disasters, was attacked by people from mainland Greece. Knossos was later rebuilt, but under new rulers - the Mycenaean Greeks.

"LINEAR A" SCRIPT DEVELOPED • CIVILIZATION DESTROYED c.1450 B.C.

THE BABYLONIANS

There was probably a settlement at Babylon from around 3000 B.C. but it did not develop into a city until after 2500 B.C. It grew thanks to its position on the River Euphrates, which was an important trade route linking the Persian Gulf to northern Mesopotamia, Syria, Anatolia, and the cities of the eastern Mediterranean coast.

By about 2000 B.C., when the Sumerian civilization was losing strength, Babylon had become the most powerful kingdom in southern Mesopotamia. It took advantage of Sumer's weakness and swept in, overpowering the old city-states. Marduk, the god worshipped in Babylon, became the most important deity in the newly founded empire of Babylonia.

The Reign of Hammurabi

Under Hammurabi, who ruled from about 1792 to 1750 B.C., Babylonian civilization reached its peak. The knowledge and myths of the Sumerians were absorbed and improved; mathematics, in particular, advanced rapidly. Perhaps the most impressive achievement, however, was the work of Hammurabi himself. He devised a long code of laws, numbering about 200 in all, covering the three classes of Babylonian society - nobles, common people, and slaves. The punishments which were handed out to those who broke the law depended upon which class the offender belonged to. If a noble broke another noble's bone, for example, the aggressor was to have one of his bones broken; if he broke a commoner's bone he paid his victim one unit of silver; and if he broke a slave's bone he paid the slave's master half of the value of the slave. Many of Hammurabi's laws governed everyday matters of trade, agriculture, and wages. The written records of the time, however, show the laws were not always obeyed.

The Defeat of Babylon

Throughout his reign, Hammurabi tried to make southern Mesopotamia a permanent, unified kingdom under the control of Babylon. He kept a very

Left: This terracotta figure of a lion-headed monster portrayed the Babylonian god Marduk.

Below: The Ishtar Gate at Babylon was built during the reign of King Nebuchadnezzar.

RISE OF BABYLONIA BEGINS 2000 B.C. • CIVILIZATION AT ITS PEAK 1792 TO 1750 B.C.

tight grip on the running of Babylonia; many of his "letters," written on clay tablets, have survived and they show how determined he was to make sure that the administration of the empire ran smoothly. When he died, there was no one who could take over this massive task, and Babylonia fell to pieces.

For the next 150 years, Babylonia was in something of a backwater, isolated from the great events taking place around it. Meanwhile, the Hittites (see pages 28-29) grew in power; in 1595 B.C. the Hittite ruler Mursilis I launched a devastating raid on Babylon. The city later became part of the Assyrian empire, although only for a short time. In about 1200 B.C., Babylon was captured by the Cassites from the Zagros Mountains to the east, and ruled by them for more than 400 years. Late in the eighth century B.C., southern Mesopotamia came under the control of the Chaldeans, tribes from the desert to the south.

In 625 B.C., Nabopolassar seized the throne of Babylon and began a vigorous campaign of conquest. Assyria was attacked, and Nineveh, the capital, was destroyed in 612 B.C. Seven years later, Nebuchadnezzar became king of Babylonia. He spent vast amounts of money restoring old religious temples and building canals. He is probably most famous for another great work of construction - the Hanging Gardens of Babylon, a huge roof garden supported on brick arches.

The rebirth of the Babylonian empire did not last long, however. Nebuchadnezzar's successor, Nabonidus, angered the powerful priests of Marduk and abandoned the throne to his son. Eventually, Babylon fell to the newly emerging Persian empire in 539 B.C.

Below: This boundary stone warned people that they were about to enter Babylonian territory.

CAPTURED BY HITTITES 1595 B.C. • NEBUCHADNEZZAR KING OF BABYLONIA 605 TO 562 B.C.

27

THE HITTITES

In the period from about 2000 to 1200 B.C., the Levant, the area around the eastern coastline of the Mediterranean Sea from the Nile in Egypt to southeast Anatolia (in what is now Turkey), was occupied by a number of independent city-states. Because they had all grown very wealthy by trading in gold, copper, and pottery, they became targets for invasion by the kingdoms in the surrounding regions, including the Egyptians, the Mitannians of northern Mesopotamia, and the Hittites of Anatolia. The Hittites had developed from a group of cities into a unified state in about 1650 B.C., and by the fourteenth century B.C. they had replaced the Mitannians as Egypt's main rivals for the Levant.

Warfare and Diplomacy

During their almost constant battles for control of the Levant, the three empires developed new ways of fighting. In around 1800 B.C., fast, two-wheeled war chariots appeared. They were very strongly built, yet light enough to be lifted by one man. Each chariot was pulled by a team of horses and manned by archers in bronze armor, who shot bronze-tipped arrows at their enemies. Many of the cities in the region had strong defensive walls, so sieges became common. Weapons such as battering rams and siege towers were invented to break down the cities' defences. In turn, the defenders devised protective ramparts with steep slopes in front of the city walls to stop attackers using their new weapons. However, even those could not prevent some cities from being overrun and destroyed.

At the same time as the wars were being fought, the various empires attempted to make peace. Clay tablets have been found, written by both the Hittites, in a language called Akkadian, and the Egyptians, in which one side or the other suggested bringing the fighting to an end.

Bogazköy

The capital of the Hittite empire was at Bogazköy, in central Anatolia. Although the surrounding area is very dry, the site for the city was chosen because water was available from a river that flowed around it. What was more, the rocky terrain formed a natural defensive barrier against attack. Bogazköy was one of the group of cities that were united as a single Hittite state in 1650 B.C. As the Hittites increased their power, they rebuilt and extended their capital. The remains of the city walls, which show how the city grew, can still be seen today. They were extremely strong, and in some places were built on top of high ramparts faced in stone. The gates that led into the city were decorated with carved lions and Hittite gods.

When archaeologists excavated the citadel at Bogazköy in 1908, they found the ruins of a royal palace, which had a massive hall 342 sq. ft., five huge temples, and two archives containing 3,000 cuneiform clay tablets. These tablets, with literary, legal, and religious texts, gave the first clue to the size and sophistication of the empire created by the Hittites. It seems that this empire, which was previously almost unknown, may have included all the lands from the Aegean Sea in the west to the Euphrates valley in the east.

The Sea Peoples

In the twelfth century B.C., all of the major states in the Levant came under attack from unknown raiders from the sea, and one by one the empires collapsed. The Hittite empire fell in around 1200 B.C., and although the Egyptians remained, their power was seriously weakened.

Below: The Lion Gate at Bogazköy, the Hittite capital.

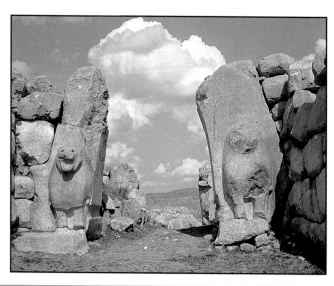

BATTLES FOR LEVANT 2000 TO 1200 B.C. • FIRST TWO-WHEELED WAR CHARIOT c.1800 B.C.

28

Below: In 1285 B.C., the Hittites defeated the Egyptians at the Battle of Kadesh and gained control of Syria.

HITTITE CITIES UNITED 1650 B.C. • HITTITES DEFEATED BY SEA PEOPLES c.1200 B.C.

MYCENAEAN GREECE

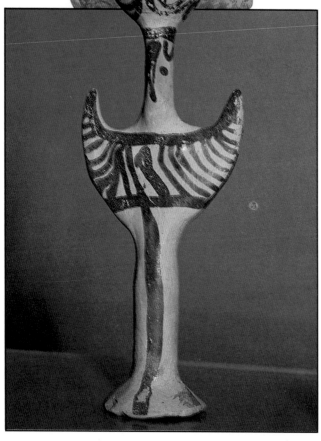

In the middle of the sixteenth century B.C., a new power emerged in the eastern Mediterranean - the state of Mycenae. It was centered on the city of Mycenae, on the Peloponnese peninsula at the southern tip of mainland Greece. Greece is a mountainous country, and a number of other states grew up on

Left: An ivory carving of a Mycenaean warrior's head. Soldier's helmets were made from the tusks of wild boar.

Below left: A terracotta figure representing a Mycenaean mother-goddess. It was made about 3,300 years ago.

Below Right: Mycenae was protected by a high stone wall. But about 1200 B.C. it was attacked and destroyed.

RISE OF MYCENAEANS c.1550 B.C. • STRONGLY INFLUENCED BY MINOAN CIVILIZATION

the fertile plains between the highlands. None of these, however, could challenge the Mycenaeans.

In some ways the Mycenaean civilization was rather like that of the Minoans. The Mycenaeans' language, a form of Greek known as "Linear B," has also been found in Crete, evidence of the fact that there was close contact between the two communities. The Mycenaeans decorated their palaces with colorful frescoes and imitated Minoan pottery designs. In other ways, however, the two civilizations were quite different. While Minoan Crete had been fairly peace loving, preferring trade to conquest, the Mycenaeans were much more warlike. Their strong

navy enabled them to control a large area of the eastern Mediterranean, while the army overpowered several neighboring Greek regions, including Attica and Boeotia, and captured Crete. They also attacked the heavily fortified citadel of Troy, on the Aegean coast of Anatolia, but without success.

Warlike Times

There is much evidence for the fact that warfare was an important part of life in Greece at this time. The city of Mycenae itself was heavily fortified, with a high stone wall up to 23 ft. thick. Other Greek citadels were also reinforced with strong defences during the Mycenaean period, which suggests that they were increasingly fearful of attack. Painted pottery and frescoes show soldiers with long spears, shields, and helmets made from the tusks of wild boars. Mycenaean warriors' tombs have been found containing vast quantities of swords and daggers, their blades often beautifully decorated with battle scenes . The armies of Mycenae used war chariots, similar to those used by other civilizations, but Greece's rugged terrain made it difficult to move chariots and men quickly. The solution to this problem was to build a network of roads throughout the Peloponnese and in the states they conquered.

Prosperity and Decline

Mycenae became a wealthy state quite quickly; one of its earliest rulers was buried in about 1550 B.C. with $11\frac{1}{4}$ lb of gold. Not all of the Mycenaeans' prosperity came from plundering other states; they also established a trading network throughout the Mediterranean. Copper and tin were imported (to make bronze), as were gold, ivory, and gemstones. Exports of pottery, bronze weapons, jewelry, olive oil, wine, and wool reached Syria, Egypt, southern Italy, and even as far as Britain.

During the thirteenth century B.C., Mycenaean power gradually began to wane, but when the end came it was swift. Invaders, possibly the Dorians of northern Greece, stormed into Mycenae's territories and destroyed its palaces. The great citadel of Mycenae itself went up in flames a short time after 1200 B.C. The invaders had no interest in civilization; writing disappeared from Greece and did not return for several centuries.

MYCENAE CONQUERS SOUTHERN GREECE • CIVILIZATION DESTROYED c.1200 B.C.

THE PHOENICIANS

The country of Phoenicia was at the eastern end of the Mediterranean, in the area known as the Levant. It occupied a narrow coastal plain some 192 mi. long and 18 mi. wide, between the sea and the mountains of Lebanon. Phoenicia consisted of a number of city-states dotted along the coast, including Tyre, Sidon, Berytus, Byblos, and Aradus. It was from these ports that the Phoenicians established a trading empire that was to cover most of the Mediterranean.

Craft and Trade

The craftsmen of Phoenicia were not particularly inventive; they took their artistic ideas from earlier civilizations, especially Egypt, and used them to produce work in bronze, ivory, wood, and textiles. When their products became popular, the craftsmen mass produced them, turning out hundreds of the same item, all with the identical pattern. Phoenician ships traveled to countries further and further afield, exchanging these products for other goods that were needed at home, such as silver, wheat, and slaves. In order to protect and increase their trade, the Phoenicians established outposts in other parts of the Mediterranean, including Carthage and Tingis in North Africa, Malaca in southern Spain, and Nora on the island of Sardinia.

But they were not to have things all their own way. From about 800 B.C., Greek city-states began to trade throughout the Aegean, the Black Sea, and much of the Mediterranean. They followed similar routes to those of the Mycenaeans before them, but were a much more powerful force to contend with. Like the Phoenicians, the Greeks set up colonies of their own - in southern Russia, Italy, eastern Spain, and elsewhere. Wherever possible, the ships of these trading empires avoided each other; the Greeks operated in the northern Mediterranean, while the Phoenicians concentrated their efforts in the south and west. Nonetheless, when their paths did cross, the two sides almost certainly fought. Phoenician warships were the most advanced of their time: they could be propelled either by wind in the sail or by oarsmen, and had a ram for piercing enemy ships.

Spreading the Word

During their trading expeditions overseas, the Phoenicians spread their culture among the peoples they came into contact with. They carried with them one particularly important gift - an alphabet.

The script which the Phoenicians developed, like many other things in their civilization, came originally from earlier times and had its roots in Egypt. Over the centuries the Egyptians' hieroglyphics had been adapted by other groups, and the Phoenicians continued this process. They created an alphabet that used only 22 signs, each of which represented a sound. This made it easy to learn and meant that

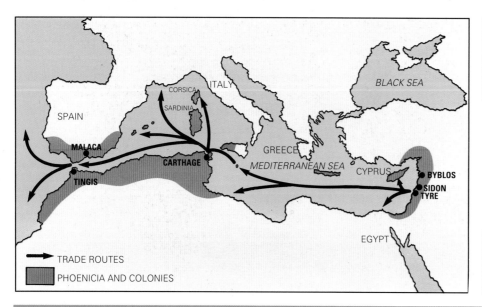

Left: From its heartland at the eastern end of the Mediterranean, Phoenicia established a large trading empire.

Right: The Phoenicians built fast warships to protect their trading ships from Greek attacks.

COLONIES IN MEDITERRANEAN 1200-800 B.C. • SIMPLE ALPHABET DEVELOPED

especially trained scribes were no longer needed.

Phoenicia's trading empire was at its height between 1200 and 800 B.C. In about 700 B.C., Tyre, their main city-state, was captured by the Assyrians and later came under the control of the Persian empire. The colony at Carthage became the center from which the southern and western Mediterranean was controlled, and it developed into an independent power that challenged first the Greeks and then the mighty Roman empire (see pages 52-53).

Below: The Phoenicians spread their language and alphabet throughout their Mediterranean trading empire.

APPEARANCE OF GREEK TRADERS AFTER 800 B.C. • ASSYRIANS CAPTURE TYRE c.700 B.C.

33

THE HEBREWS

In the second century B.C., there were many nomadic groups in the deserts of the Middle East, and the Hebrews were one of these. According to the Old Testament of the Bible, their story began with a tribal leader called Abraham, who left his home in the Sumerian city of Ur some time after 2000 B.C. and began a long journey to the country of Canaan (now called Palestine). His descendants settled there in about 1400 B.C., but following a great famine, many moved on to Egypt.

The Hebrews stayed in Egypt for several centuries. At first they lived in freedom, but were later enslaved and cruelly treated. Finally, in about 1200 B.C., they were taken out of captivity by Moses, a new leader. After Moses' death, the Hebrews crossed the Jordan River and returned to Canaan. There, they captured the city of Jericho, and then conquered the whole country.

According to the Bible, the Hebrews were guided throughout their journeys by God, whom they called Yahweh. During the time of Moses, the Hebrews' belief in a single, powerful god became more clearly defined. Traditionally, the Ten Commandments were revealed to Moses on Mount Sinai and these laws formed the basis of the "covenant," or agreement, between Yahweh and the Hebrews. Many other laws about both everyday life and worship were also written down at about this time.

The Hebrew Kings

The Hebrews were divided into 12 separate tribes. For many years, they came under attack from enemies on the borders of Canaan, especially the Philistines. They eventually decided to elect a king to lead them against their attackers. They chose Saul, who became their ruler in about 1020 B.C. When Saul was defeated in battle 20 years later, David was made king. He set up his capital at Jerusalem, in an area that did not belong to any of the 12 tribes. There were already disagreements between the tribes in the north of the country and those in the south, however, and these were to emerge again later.

David's son, Solomon, brought some prosperity to the country when he was king, mainly by increasing trade. He is also known for the buildings he constructed - cities, fortifications, and an elaborate temple at Jerusalem. After Solomon's death in about 922 B.C., the conflict between the northern and southern tribes came to a head, and the country was divided in two: the kingdom of Judah in the south, and the kingdom of Israel in the north.

Below: The Ark of the Covenant - the symbol of God's presence - is carried into Jerusalem.

MOSES LEADS HEBREWS OUT OF EGYPT c.1200 B.C. • SAUL BECOMES KING c.1020 B.C.

34

Far right: Jews inside the Masada fortress held out against Roman attacks during A.D. 72 and 73.

Right: Baal was regarded by Hebrews as a "false god;" they worshiped Yahweh.

The Fall of Judah

From about 600 B.C., the Hebrew lands were invaded by empires beyond their borders. Israel was conquered by the Assyrians in 721 B.C., and Judah was dominated first by Egypt and then by the Babylonians, who finally destroyed Jerusalem in 587 B.C. Many Hebrews were taken as captives to Babylon. When the Persians defeated the Babylonians in 539 B.C., they gave permission for the Hebrews, or Israelites, to return to their land. The returning exiles came to be known as Jews.

After Persian rule, the Israelites became part of Alexander the Great's empire (see pages 56-57), and were later governed by Egypt and then the Seleucids. Finally, in 164 B.C., Jerusalem was retaken by the Jews, only to be captured once more, in 63 B.C., by the Romans. From 34 B.C., the land was ruled on behalf of the Romans by King Herod. It was during Herod's reign that Jesus Christ was born.

During the first two centuries A.D., the Jewish people rebelled several times against the Romans. In A.D. 70, the Romans destroyed the temple in Jerusalem, and many Jews fled to other countries. In A.D. 135, the Roman emperor established the colony of Aelia Capitoliana on the site of ruined Jerusalem. Only non-Jews were allowed to live there.

ISRAELITES EXILED IN BABYLON 587-539 B.C. • TEMPLE DESTROYED A.D. 70

EARLY AMERICA

Humans probably first entered North America around 40,000 years ago from Siberia. At that time, the level of the sea was lower than it is today, and people could walk across the "land bridge" between the two continents. By 9000 B.C., there were groups of hunter-gatherers as far south as the tip of South America. About 1,000 years later, native plants, such as beans, corn, pumpkins, and cotton, were being cultivated, and the first agricultural villages grew up around 3000 B.C.

Below: A statue of a Mayan nobleman from Jaina island, off the Yucatan.

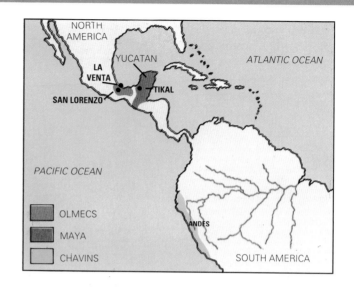

Above: The civilizations of the Olmecs, the Maya and the Chavíns.

Below: A temple at the Mayan city of Tikal.

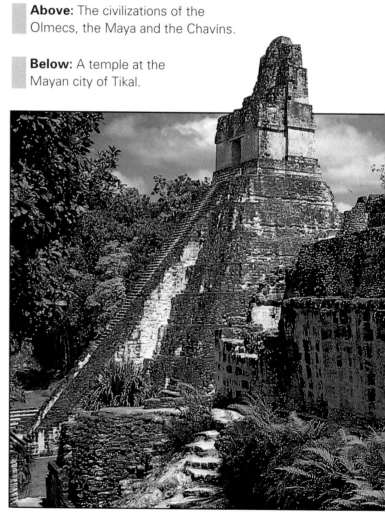

GROWTH OF OLMEC AND CHAVÍN CIVILIZATIONS FROM 1200 B.C. • OLMECS FALL 300 B.C.

The Olmecs and the Chavíns

The first important American civilizations developed around 1200 B.C. They were the Olmecs, who lived in Central America, and the Chavíns of the Andes mountains in Peru.

The first Olmec capital was at San Lorenzo, on the Gulf Coast of what is now Mexico, but when this was destroyed in 900 B.C., La Venta became the major city. In the center of La Venta was a huge clay pyramid, 11½ ft. high, with large open spaces, or plazas, on either side. The pyramid was probably built for religious ceremonies. Olmec gods were fierce-looking beings which were part-human and part-animal - eagles, snakes, and especially jaguars were all shown on religious carvings.

The Olmecs were probably a warlike people - some of their monuments show carvings of armed men - although they do not seem to have set out to build a vast empire. They traded with the peoples in the surrounding region to obtain the raw materials they could not get locally, including jade, basalt (a

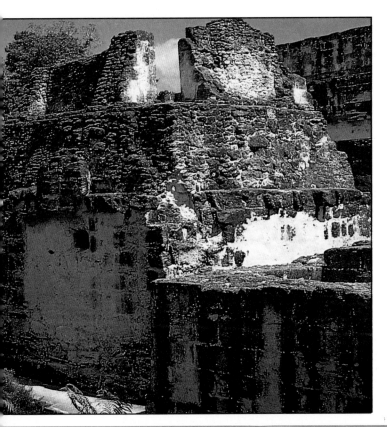

hard type of stone), and obsidian (volcanic glass). A form of hieroglyphic writing was invented by the Olmecs, and they also devised a system of numbers. Their civilization came to an end around 300 B.C. when La Venta was attacked and abandoned; it is not known who destroyed it.

At the same time as the Olmecs were living in Central America, the Chavíns were developing their own culture high up in the Andes in South America. Like the Olmecs, the Chavíns worshiped gods which were part-animal and part-human. They may have used shells in their religious ceremonies, because large conch shells and thorny oyster shells have been found in the area which they ruled. Other finds include painted textiles, wood and stone carvings, gold and silver ornaments, and pottery.

The Maya

Perhaps the most famous early civilization of Central America is that of the Maya, who lived in what is now Guatemala from about 2000 B.C. Very little was known about them until 30 years ago, when their hieroglyphic writing was first deciphered.

The Mayan civilization reached its peak between 300 B.C. and A.D. 800. During this time large cities were built, with plazas and stone pyramids, palaces, and temples. The main cities housed up to 50,000 people, who were fed with produce from the fields nearby, including corn, root vegetables, beans, and chili peppers. These large cities were mainly centers of government and religion. Other cities seem to have been ruled by dynasties of kings, and were constantly at war with one another to obtain victims for human sacrifice - an important part of Mayan religious ceremonies.

Mayan artists were very skilled at pottery, wall painting, and wood and stone carving. The most valuable material to the Maya was jade, which was carved to make beads and other jewelry.

The Maya began to decline from around A.D. 850, when many cities were abandoned. New cities were built in part of their territory, but these were destroyed during civil wars that broke out in the middle of the fifteenth century. By the time Spanish invaders started to appear, after 1517, only a few small towns were left standing.

THE CELTS

Celtic people may have lived in Europe for several thousand years before the birth of Christ, but it was not until about 800 B.C. that they developed a culture of their own. Most of what we now know about them comes from the graves in which they were buried, the remains of their fortresses, and their art.

Iron Age Europe

The technique of making tools and weapons from iron played an important part in Celtic culture. It was first discovered in western Asia between 2000 and 1500 B.C., but soon spread in all directions, reaching central Europe in around 1000 B.C. and Britain 300 years later. At first iron goods were quite rare and expensive. The ore from which iron is made is plentiful in Europe, however, and slowly the new metal replaced bronze. Iron swords and other weapons came first, followed by tools and other everyday objects. The metal was heated until it became soft, beaten into the shape that was required, and then allowed to cool.

Because iron is harder than bronze, its discovery changed the way in which war was fought. Tougher, sharper weapons were more effective than bronze ones and, as ironworking spread, more people could be equipped with them. Iron could also be used to strengthen defences. It is believed, for example, that the timber ramparts of one Celtic settlement, Manching in Bavaria, were held in position using 300 tons of iron nails. The use of iron even affected the

Below: Many Celts lived in farms and villages grouped around a hill fort or fortified town.

Left: From southern Germany and the Alps, the Celts spread throughout much of Europe.

FIRST USE OF IRON IN EUROPE c.1000 B.C. • RISE OF CELTIC CULTURE c.800 B.C.

Above: Maiden Castle. Celts in Britain built huge hill forts like this one to protect themselves from attack.

landscape of Europe: with sharp iron tools, large areas of forest could be cut down to make room for settlements and increase agricultural land.

The Spread of Celtic Culture

The early heartland of the Celts was in southern Germany and the eastern Alps. From about 800 B.C., the Celts began to expand their territory. By 500 B.C., Celtic-speaking people had settled in France and Spain; by 400 B.C., they had moved into parts of Italy and attacked Rome in 390 B.C.; and by 275 B.C., they had reached Greece and Anatolia. At some time after 450 B.C., the Celts reached Britain, although the exact date is not known.

During the same period in which the Celts were spreading outward, other important changes were taking place among them. They came into contact with the peoples of the Mediterranean - especially in the overseas colonies set up by the Greeks - and this led to a rapid increase in trade. From this time, Celtic nobles were buried with fine, valuable objects imported from other countries.

The Celts themselves were excellent craftsmen. The graves of chieftains, princesses, and other rich people contained beautiful bronze vessels used for pouring and drinking wine, gold neck rings, and decorated sword sheaths.

In about 300 B.C., the Celts began to use coins, which were similar in design to the Greek money of the time. Around 150 years later, large fortified sites, called *oppida*, started to appear. They were rather like small towns, with timber houses, barns, storehouses, and workshops where bronze and iron goods, pottery, textiles, and coins were made.

The Celts continued to trade with the Mediterranean, although their earlier Greek trading partners had by this time been replaced by the Romans. Within a short time, the Celts were to suffer Roman influence of a different kind. As Rome grew, not even the heavily fortified hilltop sites could protect the Celts. By 100 B.C., southern France had become a Roman colony, and within 250 years most of the remaining Celtic territory had been captured. Only Ireland and northern Scotland stayed beyond the Romans' grasp, and Celtic culture survived there until the Middle Ages.

TRADE WITH GREEK COLONIES FROM 600 B.C. • CELTS FALL TO ROMANS BY A.D. 150

THE ETRUSCANS

In about 800 B.C., a remarkable civilization began in Italy, in the fertile area between the Tiber River, the Po River, and the Apennine Mountains. Much of this region is still known as Tuscany, after the Etruscan people who lived there.

No one knows for sure where the Etruscans came from. They may have been local people who developed their culture through contact with Greek traders, or they could have come from western Asia after the collapse of the Hittite and Mycenaean empires. Whatever their origins, they were to have an important effect on the history of Italy.

Cities, Trade, and Culture

The first signs of Etruscan civilization were two groups of prosperous cities that grew up, one in the north and the other to the south. Both groups depended on agriculture, although the southern cities seem also to have had strong trading links with other lands, especially Greece.

Vases and other works of art were imported, while bronze and black pottery (known as *bucchero*) were exported. The Etruscans were highly skilled in the creation of bronze pots, brooches, mirrors, and candelabra, and the statues that they made from terracotta were also extremely popular.

Greeks had settled in southern Italy much earlier, and the Etruscans took advantage of this to extend their trade southward. However, traders transporting goods along this route frequently came under attack from hill tribes. The Etruscans' overseas trade was also badly hit in 474 B.C. when they were defeated by the Carthaginians in a sea battle at Cumae, near what is now Naples.

Apart from their own achievements, the Etruscans are important because of the part they played in the growth of Roman civilization. Their engineering skills - they built impressive road networks, canals, and underground tunnels to carry rivers *under* roads - had a direct influence on early Rome. Their religion, with its complex group of humanlike gods, was also echoed later by Roman ideas.

We know very little about how Etruscan cities were run. This is mainly because no one has yet been able to understand the Etruscan language fully. Although the characters used were very similar to those of the Greek alphabet, the language itself is unlike any other known today. Scholars have been able to translate some simple texts found on tomb paintings, but the few long texts which still exist are not really understood.

The End of the Etruscans

The decline of the Etruscan civilization, from around 300 B.C., was caused partly by the fact that their cities were never truly united. The main reason, however, was the rapid growth of the civilization to the south of their lands - Rome.

As Rome increased in power, it was able to control the Etruscans' trade routes. The Romans also conquered the city of Veii and forced Caere to become their ally, after which the remaining Etruscan cities fell

Below: A Greek vase found at the city of Vulci. Many vases and other works of art were imported by the Etruscans.

one by one under the power of Rome. This process happened quite gradually; there was not any all-out wars, although there were occasional battles. The Etruscans came to realize that their future was tied to that of Rome, and they attempted to make the best of their situation. By about 100 B.C., all the main Etruscan cities were part of the Roman republic. The Etruscans had played an important part in the development of Roman civilization, and in the end that great and powerful civilization took them over.

Below: Many Etruscan tombs were built like underground houses where the dead could live in the after life.

Right: The Etruscan civilization developed around Cumae in southern Italy and Veii and Caere in the north.

RIVER PO

RIVER TIBER

MEDITERRANEAN SEA

VEII

CAERE

ROME

ITALY

CUMAE

ORIGINAL ETRUSCAN TERRITORY

ETRUSCAN EXPANSION

GREEK COLONIES

INFLUENCED ROMAN CIVILIZATION • ABSORBED BY ROME c.300 TO100 B.C.

THE ASSYRIANS

Following the collapse of the Hittite empire and the decline of the Egyptians around 1200 B.C., the city-states which were scattered throughout Mesopotamia and the Levant were once again independent. They were not, however, to remain so for very long.

The Rise of Assyria

The state of Assyria first emerged in about 2360 B.C., and was grouped around the heavily fortified city of Ashur, on the Tigris River. In time, the Assyrians captured lands to the west and extended their rule as far as the coast of the Mediterranean. They were not, however, able to hold their possessions for long and their territory shrank back to a small area around Ashur. By 911 B.C., Assyrian kings were once again leading their armies on raids to capture more land. Their conquests began under King Adadnirari II and his grandson, Ashurnasirpal II, and the Assyrian empire reached its height under Sargon II in the late eighth century B.C. At that time it included the

BIRTH OF ASSYRIAN STATE c.2360 B.C. • EMPIRE REACHES ITS PEAK c.721 TO 705 B.C.

Assyrian heartland around Ashur, the Levantine city-states, Syria, Palestine, Cyprus, and, to the west, parts of Anatolia.

In 880 B.C., the Assyrian capital had been moved from Ashur to Nimrud and by the time Sargon became king (721 B.C.) it had moved again, this time to Khorsabad. From the stone carvings, called reliefs, which decorated the royal palaces in the capitals, we can see how the Assyrians were able to conquer so much territory. They were remarkably inventive in warfare: the palace reliefs show several different types of infantry, armored cavalry, horse-drawn chariots with shield bearers and archers, and soldiers besieging cities by digging tunnels and using battering rams and ladders.

In order to hold on to their possessions, the Assyrians divided their empire into provinces, each ruled by a governor and occupied by soldiers. Conquered states and cities were forced to pay the Assyrians money to prevent further attack, and this was one source of the empire's great wealth. The coastal cities of the Levant provided more in the form of harbor taxes on cargoes, and were also used to import luxury goods. The Taurus Mountains in Anatolia were rich in iron, lead, and copper, while the fertile crop-growing lands of Mesopotamia fed the towns and cities of Assyria and its armies.

The Rise and Fall of Nineveh

Around the end of Sargon's reign (705 B.C.,) the capital moved again, this time to Nineveh. The city became the greatest of all the Assyrian capitals, dominated by a huge citadel containing palaces and temples. The royal palace had a network of throne rooms and reception halls where court officials, foreign ambassadors, and conquered leaders were received. Nearby was the royal arsenal, where both military equipment and goods plundered during conquest were stored.

As well as being the most impressive Assyrian capital, Nineveh was also the last. Not surprisingly, the empire had many enemies. Chief among these were the Babylonians to the south, under their new king Nabopolassar, the Scythians to the north, and the Medes to the east. At the end of the seventh century B.C. these forces joined to overthrow the

Assyrian empire. Nineveh and Nimrud were destroyed in 612 B.C. and the power of the Assyrians fell with them. The structure of their empire lived on, however, and was taken over by the Babylonians.

Below: A winged, human-headed bull, which guarded the entrance to Khorsabad.

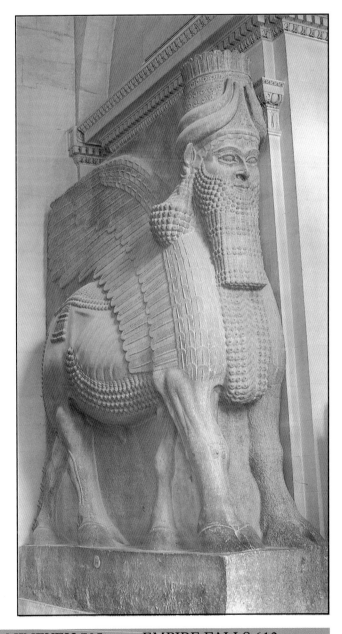

CAPITAL MOVES FROM KHORSABAD TO NINEVEH 705 B.C. • EMPIRE FALLS 612 B.C.

43

ARCHAIC GREECE

Several centuries after the power of the Mycenaeans declined in about 1100 B.C., a number of small city-states grew up in the fertile plains between the mountains of Greece, on the islands of the Aegean Sea, and in the lands that bordered the sea. Each city-state had its own king, government, and laws, and often its own army, too. Around the central city, or *polis*, were the farms and villages of the ordinary people, who lived by growing corn, vegetables, and olives, and rearing goats for milk and cheese.

The Greek World

The Greek city-states were all independent, and were only linked by the fact that their citizens all spoke Greek and worshiped Greek gods. One innovation that increased their links was the Olympic Games, which were first held in 776 B.C., and in which people from all over the Greek world participated. Another was money in the form of coins, which was invented in about 600 B.C. The first coins were made of electrum - a mixture of gold and silver - but later they were solid silver. Although most people still bartered, that is exchanged one type of goods for another, coins came to be used by traders for buying and selling. Some of the first silver coins were made in Athens; on one side they had a picture of an owl, the symbol of Athena, the goddess of the city.

From about 750 B.C., ships from the Greek city-states began to sail to other regions. They carried people who were searching for land of their own, or who were simply hoping to trade. Cities such as Corinth, Eretria, and Megara set up colonies in southern Italy, Spain, North Africa, around the Black Sea, and in southwest Anatolia. Some of these colonies are still important cities today - Naples in Italy, and Marseille in France, for example. In this way, Greek culture was spread throughout the Mediterranean region.

Athens, Sparta, and Persia

By the fifth century B.C., two states - Athens and Sparta - had become extremely powerful. At first they stood together in order to fight off the armies of Persia. In 490 B.C., the huge Persian empire launched an attack on Athens. Their ships put ashore an army of 20,000 men, but in the battle of Marathon which followed, the Greeks triumphed. Ten years later, a much larger Persian army was ready to attack again. It was so large that it could not be transported across the Aegean by ship. Instead the soldiers marched overland toward Greece, keeping close to the shore so that food and other supplies could be carried to

Below: A Greek infantryman from between 600 and 500 B.C.

EMERGENCE OF GREEK CITY-STATES c.800 B.C. • FIRST OLYMPIC GAMES HELD 776 B.C.

44

them by sea. The Greeks realized that if the Persian navy was destroyed, the army would be weakened. While the advance of the Persian army was being delayed by the Spartans, the Persians' ships were lured to the island of Salamis, where, in 480 B.C., most of them were sunk or scattered by the Athenian navy. The Persian king Xerxes could only watch helplessly as his fleet was destroyed.

Despite their cooperation against the Persians, by 431 B.C. Sparta and Athens were fighting each other in the Peloponnesian War, which lasted 27 years. The war was a disaster for Athens. After years of stalemate, the balance tilted in Sparta's favor when the great Persian empire began supplying it with money to build new ships. The Spartan commander, Lysander, defeated the Athenian navy and then besieged Athens itself. Unable to obtain food, the Athenians starved through the winter of 405 B.C. and surrendered the following spring.

Above: Some of the main Greek city-states. Each had its own king and government.

Below: Wrestling was a popular sport in Greece; it helped soldiers keep fit and strong for battle.

GREECE ATTACKED BY PERSIANS 490 B.C. • ATHENS AND SPARTA AT WAR 431 TO 404 B.C.

45

THE RED SEA STATES

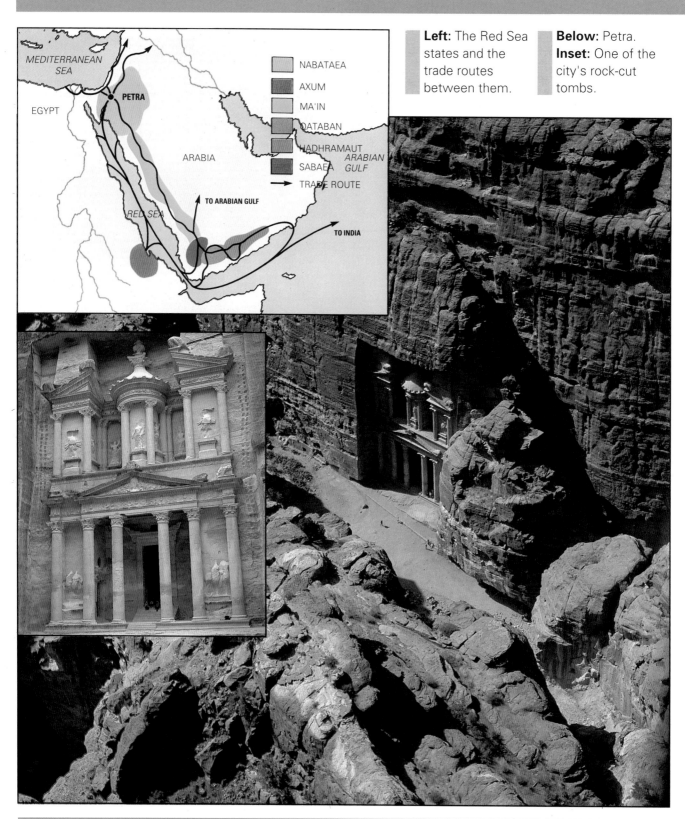

Map legend:
- NABATAEA
- AXUM
- MA'IN
- QATABAN
- HADHRAMAUT
- SABAEA
- → TRADE ROUTE

Map labels: MEDITERRANEAN SEA, EGYPT, PETRA, ARABIA, ARABIAN GULF, RED SEA, TO ARABIAN GULF, TO INDIA

Left: The Red Sea states and the trade routes between them.

Below: Petra.
Inset: One of the city's rock-cut tombs.

RISE OF SOUTHERN ARABIAN STATES AND NABATAEA ON INCENSE ROUTE c.550 B.C.

During the 600 years before the birth of Christ, the Red Sea - between northeast Africa and Arabia - and the lands around it, were an important corridor for trade. A number of wealthy kingdoms grew up in this region, including the so-called "incense states" of southern Arabia (Sabaea, Qataban, Hadhramaut, and Ma'in), Axum in Ethiopia, and Nabataea, at the northeast end of the Red Sea.

The reason for the prosperity of these kingdoms was the fact that they controlled the overland trade between southern Arabia and the eastern Mediterranean. The most important of the goods traded were frankincense and myrrh - aromatic substances which were grown in the south and exported to Egypt, the Near East, Greece, and Rome to be used in a variety of religious ceremonies, embalming, perfumes, and cosmetics.

The Incense States

Frankincense and myrrh are gums which are obtained when the bark of certain species of tree is cut. The gum is allowed to harden and is then collected. It gives off a pleasant smell when it is burned and is still used today.

Southern Arabia is extremely dry and so the incense states built impressive irrigation systems to keep their valuable trees and food crops watered. The state of Hadhramaut was the main source of frankincense. When the hardened gum had been gathered, it was transported through several states on its way to the eastern Mediterranean. It passed first through Qataban and Sabaea, then through Ma'in, which lay along the Red Sea coast. When the trade first began, the incense was carried by asses, but these were later replaced by camels, which can travel for long periods without needing water. The roads were mainly dusty desert tracks, although they were paved in some places, especially over mountain passes. At various points along the route the road was blocked so that tolls could be collected. Not much of the incense trade went by ship because the Red Sea was very difficult to navigate. When people came to understand the seasonal monsoon winds that blew in the region, however, more goods were sent by sea. The Ethiopian state of Axum, with its trading port at Adulis, grew up as a result.

Above: Frankincense trees being cultivated in modern-day Oman.

Nabataea

The final state through which the camel caravans passed before reaching the Mediterranean Sea was Nabataea. Petra, its capital, was carved out of the red sandstone rocks of the mountains. It was situated in a valley surrounded by cliffs and the desert, and very little food could be grown there. Yet, by around 100 B.C., 30,000 people lived in Petra, thanks to its vital position on the incense trade route. A complex system of earthenware pipes and storage tanks brought drinking water from mountain springs into the heart of the city.

The Nabataeans built spectacular tombs for their kings. These were cut into the rock between about 100 B.C. and A.D. 150, when the city was at its height. The fronts of some of these tombs are Greek in style, showing Petra's links with the Mediterranean world. In A.D. 106 Petra was annexed by the Romans, who added various other buildings, including a theater.

In the second and third centuries A.D., the overland routes were used less and less as sea trade increased. Finally, Petra lost its reason for existence, and in about A.D. 550 it was abandoned.

ROCK TOMBS OF PETRA c.100 B.C. TO A.D. 150 • PETRA ABANDONED c. A.D. 550

AFRICAN CIVILIZATIONS

About 10,000 years ago, the area that is now the Sahara Desert was not desert at all, but wet grassland on which farmers herded cattle and grew wheat and barley. After about 2500 B.C., the climate changed and the grasslands started to dry out. As a result, the farmers moved south into tropical Africa to find new crop-growing areas. There they began cultivating millet, sorghum (a type of cereal grass), and yams; in places where the land was covered with dense forest, the people lived principally by fishing instead of farming.

The first civilization to develop in subSaharan Africa, that is Africa south of the Sahara and Egypt, was the kingdom of Kush on the banks of the Nile, in what is now Ethiopia. From about 600 B.C., Meroë, its capital, was an important center for ironworking. Kush was eventually invaded and conquered by an army from Axum (see pages 46-47) in about A.D. 350.

Africa in the Iron Age

One of the most important events in the development of the rest of subSaharan Africa was the manufacture of iron, which began there in around 600 B.C. In most other civilizations, copper and bronze had been made before ironworking was discovered, but in Africa people seem to have gone straight from using stone tools to making iron ones. Ironworking technology was probably brought from the Phoenician colonies on the North African coast, rather than from Kush, and carried across the Sahara along trade routes from the Mediterranean.

Among the first Africans to manufacture iron were the Nok people, who had lived in what is now the west African state of Nigeria since about 900 B.C. Among the few remains of Nok culture are a number of terracotta heads, some of which are life sized and were clearly modeled on real people. They were probably used for religious rituals.

The Spread of Agriculture

People living in west Africa - including, perhaps, those of the Nok culture - began to move into other parts of Africa from around 500 B.C. As they did so, they spread their language, Bantu, and their iron-working skills. Some moved south through what is now Zaïre to Namibia, while others settled around Lake Victoria in the east. The manufacture of iron was quickly taken up by the farming communities who were already living in these areas.

Bantu-speakers continued to spread south in the first few centuries A.D. and they introduced iron-working to southern Africa. They also took with them knowledge of another important technique - farming. The inhabitants of southern Africa, including the San and Khoi-khoi peoples, were hunter-gatherers. The Bantu-speakers steadily laid claim to the most fertile lands they found and either pushed out or absorbed the native populations. Eventually, farmers using iron tools spread throughout southern Africa, except for the far southwest, which was too dry for crop growing.

By about A.D. 1000, most of the peoples of sub-Saharan Africa lived in settled farming communities,

Left: This rock painting was done by people living in the Sahara Desert around 8,000 years ago.

KINGDOM OF KUSH EMERGES c.900 B.C. • IRON-WORKING IN WEST AFRICA c.600 B.C.

and the first powerful states, such as Ghana in the west, and Zimbabwe in the east, had begun to emerge. These new states depended on trade: gold, ivory, and slaves were exported in return for glass, porcelain, silk, beads, and shells. The main trading partners, especially in east Africa, were Arab merchants, some of whom settled along the coast.

From the fifteenth century, however, a new influence appeared in Africa - Europeans. Coming from Portugal, Britain, Holland, France, Belgium, and other countries in Europe, they first established trading networks and then claimed possession of the entire continent. By 1913, there was hardly an area of Africa that was not part of an European empire.

Below: A dwelling hut made from grass laid over a wooden frame.

Right: The spread of Bantu-speaking peoples and ironworking in Africa.

BANTU-SPEAKERS SPREAD FARMING AND USE OF IRON SOUTHWARD FROM 500 B.C.

ACHAEMENID PERSIA

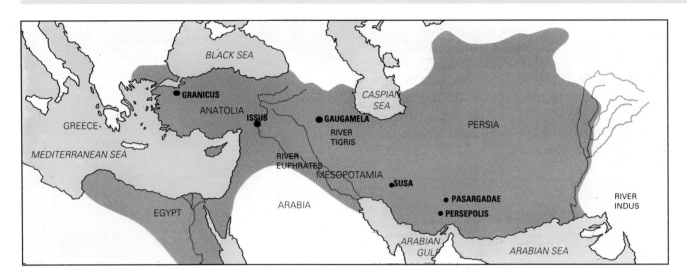

Above: The vast Persian empire at its height in about 550 B.C.

During the sixth century B.C., the largest empire the world had ever seen came into existence - the Achaemenid empire of Persia. Its name comes from Archaemenes, an early Persian king. Until the middle of the sixth century the Persians had not played a major part in the affairs of western Asia, but had been overshadowed by their much more powerful northern neighbors, the Medes.

Conquest and Decline

In 559 B.C., Cyrus II, a brilliant young king, came to the throne in Persia. He managed to unite scattered Persian and Iranian groups and rebelled against the Medes. After a hard-fought war, Cyrus triumphed, and, in 550 B.C., annexed the Median empire to form the Persian empire.

During the following 11 years, Cyrus attacked and defeated the Lydians and Ionians in western Anatolia, and the Babylonians. Finally, his empire extended to the borders of Egypt in the west and to the Indus River in the east. Nomadic tribes were mounting raids in the eastern part of the empire, however, and in 529 B.C. Cyrus was killed while fighting against them. His successor, Cambyses II, conquered Egypt in 525 B.C. but died three years later on his way back to Persia to deal with a revolt inside the empire. Darius, an army general, became king and crushed the rebellion before setting off to expand the empire still further. He invaded Greece in 490 B.C. but his army was defeated at the Battle of Marathon (see pages 44-45).

In 486 B.C., Darius was succeeded by his son Xerxes, who assembled a huge force to renew the Persians' attempts to capture Greece. At first he was successful, defeating the Spartans at Thermopylae, but disaster struck when more than half of his navy was sunk at Salamis in 480 B.C. After this, Xerxes lost interest in conquering Greece and withdrew to one of his palaces, where he was assassinated in 465 B.C.

The Persian empire went into a steady decline over the next 130 years. The days of conquest were over and the army was more often involved in subduing rebellions - in Anatolia, Egypt, Palestine, and elsewhere. The beginning of the end came when Philip of Macedon took control of Greece. Alexander the Great, Philip's son and successor, invaded Persia in 334 B.C., and in the Battle of Issus (333 B.C.) and the Battle of Gaugamela (331 B.C.) defeated Darius III, the last Achaemenid. In 330 B.C., he captured Persepolis, one of the main cities of the empire. Darius III was murdered in the same year.

Power and Glory

The remains of several Persian royal palaces have survived, but only those at Persepolis, Susa, and Pasargadae have been excavated by archaeologists. Their huge size and the beauty of their sculpted

CYRUS CREATES PERSIAN EMPIRE 559 TO 529 B.C. • DEFEAT IN GREECE 490 AND 480 B.C.

decorations show how wealthy the empire was. One carved relief at Persepolis depicts people from 23 different conquered lands bringing gifts to the king. Among the gifts were clothing, gold, elephant tusks, and exotic animals such as antelope and okapi. A hoard of 170 gold and silver objects, known as the Oxus Treasure, has been found near what was the eastern border of the Persian empire. It includes beautifully made gold armlets, a model war chariot, and engraved sword sheaths.

The conquest and administration of such a large empire was extremely costly and, although we do not know much about how the ordinary people lived, there is no doubt that they were taxed heavily. But the Achaemenid kings did not simply conquer and rule; they spent large sums of money on increasing the prosperity of captured lands. In 500 B.C. they are thought to have built a canal linking the Nile to the Red Sea, and they also created vast irrigation schemes in the east.

Right and below: The ruins of the great Persian palace at Persepolis, and a carved stone relief from one of the palace walls.

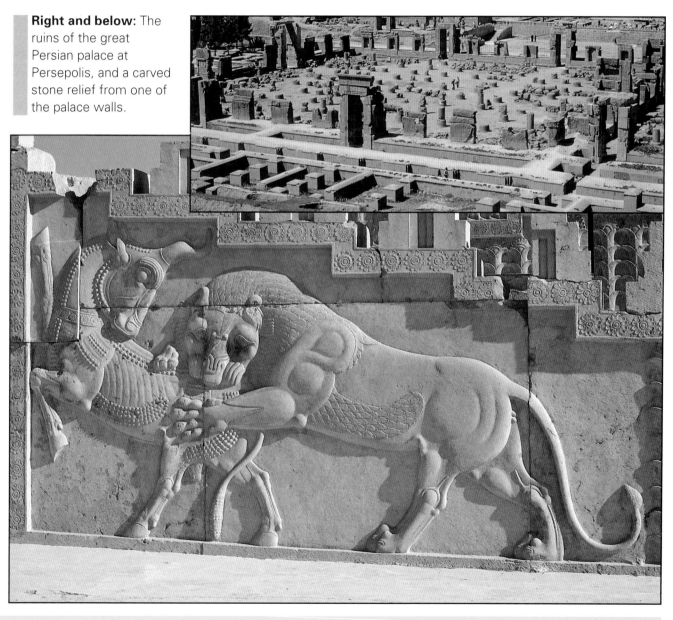

BATTLE OF GAUGAMELA 331 B.C. • DARIUS III KILLED 330 B.C.

THE CARTHAGINIANS

The city of Carthage, on the coast of what is now Tunisia, was founded in about 814 B.C. by the Phoenicians (see pages 32-33). Its purpose was to protect the Phoenicians' trade routes between their own cities on the eastern Mediterranean coast and Spain. During the sixth century B.C., the Phoenician cities were captured first by the Babylonians and then the Persians, and Phoenician settlements on Sicily came under attack from the Greeks. Carthage went to the aid of the Sicilian settlements, and further increased its power by joining the Etruscans to defeat the Greeks in a sea battle in 535 B.C.

The Carthaginian Empire

By the end of the sixth century B.C., Carthage was an independent state, and was tied to the original Phoenician cities only by having the same religion. In the century that followed, the Carthaginians created an empire of their own and became the most powerful force in the western Mediterranean.

The empire was created to defend the Carthaginians' trade, and it was trade that brought the empire its prosperity. The major sources of wealth were silver and tin from Spain, and gold from Africa. Carthage also traded with the Greeks in the Aegean and in Sicily, probably selling them food. Goods manufactured in Carthage were doubtless sold abroad, although the city's craftsmen were not especially original or skilful.

In the early days of the empire, Carthage's main rivals were the Greeks, who attempted to capture its settlements and trade routes. The Carthaginians quickly raised large armies of mercenaries - paid foreign soldiers - to fight off the Greek threat.

Carthage and Rome

The most serious threat, however, was to come from Rome. After the Carthaginians had dominated the western Mediterranean for 300 years, they came face to face with the might of the Roman republic. The two powers had signed treaties in 508 and 348 B.C., recognizing each other's authority over certain territories and trade routes. But as Rome expanded further and further, peace could not last. Of the three Punic Wars between Rome and Carthage, the first was fought mainly on and around Sicily from 264 to 241 B.C. When peace terms were signed, Carthage gave up Sicily and Sardinia.

| Above right: | The route of Hannibal's great journey during the Second Punic War (218-201 B.C.). |

Right: Hannibal led his army across the Alps in 218 B.C. and then beat the Romans several times in battle.

The Second Punic War (218-201 B.C.) began rather better for the Carthaginians, when Hannibal, one of their generals, marched an army from Spain, through the Alps, and almost to the gates of Rome. His army used elephants in battle and partly thanks to these four-legged "tanks," he was able to score some dramatic victories. He was fighting a long way from home, however, and could not always get the supplies and reinforcements he needed.

A great commander, Hannibal managed to control his army in enemy territory for 15 years before being beaten by the sheer size of the Roman army. Rome took over most of Spain in 206 B.C., and Hannibal returned to Africa in 203 B.C. - that was one of the terms of the peace treaty. Scipio, a Roman general, inflicted the final defeat upon Hannibal at the battle of Zama in 202 B.C. Carthage was forced to surrender its fleet and all its overseas territories.

On his return to Africa, Hannibal became the leader of Carthage and attempted to make it a more unified state. This aroused the suspicion of the Romans, who forced him into exile and constantly pursued him. He committed suicide in 183 B.C. rather than allow himself to be captured.

Rome also became alarmed when Carthage once again began to build up its trade. In the Third Punic War, which began in 149 B.C., the Romans were determined to put an end to Carthage. Three years later they succeeded: the city was captured and completely destroyed in 146 B.C.

Right: This is all that remains of the city of Carthage.

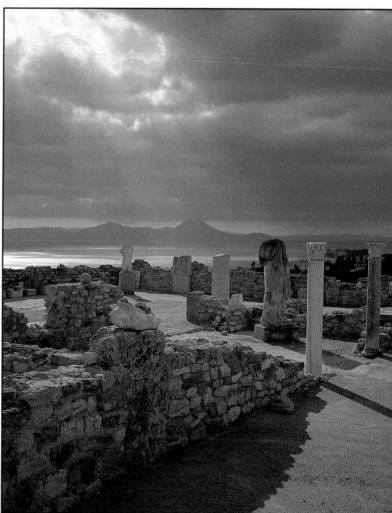

FIRST PUNIC WAR 264 TO 241 B.C. • SECOND 218 TO 201 B.C. • THIRD 149 TO 146 B.C.

CLASSICAL GREECE

In the fifth century B.C., Athens became the most important city-state in Greece and the entire Mediterranean. Despite its defeat at the hands of the Spartans (see pages 44-45), it held onto its position of prestige for more than 400 years. Throughout this time, known as the Classical period, Athens was the cultural and intellectual center of the known world.

Classical Civilization

Among the greatest achievements of Classical Greece were the many advances that were made in sculpture and architecture. These two art forms were joined together in one stunning creation - the Parthenon temple. When the Persian army attacked Athens in 480 B.C., they destroyed the Temple of Athena which stood on the Acropolis, the steep hill in the center of the city. The Parthenon was built in 462 B.C., to replace that temple. It was constructed entirely from local marble - including even the roof tiles - and was one of the largest temples in Greece. A carved frieze ran around the top of the main building facing the external columns. This showed scenes from the life of the goddess Athena, and from the procession that took place in her honor, the Panathenaia.

Some years later, the Theatre of Dionysus was built below the Acropolis. It was there that the works of the great Athenian playwrights, such as Sophocles and Aristophanes, were performed. Their plays - tragedies, comedies, and histories - often centered around the events and heroes of Greek myths.

In the Classical period, science also developed. Great strides were made in medicine and in mathematics. Greek philosophers, such as Socrates, Plato, and Aristotle, wrote about the Universe and the place of humans within it; for the first time people were regarded as individuals with their own destinies.

Religion

The Greeks worshiped many gods and goddesses, and had hundreds of legends about their lives and deeds. There were local gods and other, more important, ones who looked after every aspect of life and death. According to legend, the first gods were created by Mother Earth and were known as Titans. In Classical times, the most important gods, including Zeus, who ruled over all the others, were thought to live on Mount Olympus in northeast Greece.

Above: Pericles was the most important statesman of Classical Greece.

Below: The Panathenaia procession was held to honor the goddess Athena.

PARTHENON TEMPLE BUILT 462 B.C. • BEGINNINGS OF DEMOCRACY IN ATHENS

The Birth of Democracy

The homes of the ordinary Athenians were nothing like the splendid public buildings that were constructed in Classical times. Most people lived in small houses with bare earth floors, grouped around courtyards. The streets were narrow and unpaved, and there was not an adequate sewage system.

However, the citizens of Athens benefited in another way from the age in which they lived. Unlike other city-states, Athens gave its people a right to influence how they were governed. The city was ruled by an assembly which was elected by the people, and citizens were allowed to speak to the assembly about any matter they chose. Public figures who were thought to be too powerful or not doing their job properly could be expelled by the voters. This was not true democracy, because only male citizens over 18 years old had political rights - women, slaves, and non-Athenians were not allowed to vote. But it was the first step toward the system of government we know today.

One man, Pericles, became effectively the head of the Athenian government. The people trusted his advice and reelected him every year from about 443 until his death in 429 B.C.

RISE OF CLASSICAL DRAMA, ART, PHILOSOPHY, AND SCIENCE

THE MACEDONIANS

The land of Macedonia, to the north of Greece, was a tribal kingdom until the beginning of the fourth century B.C. It was not very unified and, because of that, was frequently attacked by its neighbors.

The Rule of Philip

The man who did most to build up the power of Macedonia was Philip, who came to power in 359 B.C., when he was made regent to govern on behalf of a new king who was too young to rule. Philip quickly took the throne himself and, after first strengthening his army, defeated the neighboring kingdoms, creating a stronghold from which he could conquer lands further afield. By 339 B.C. the Macedonian empire stretched from the River Danube in the north to the Aegean Sea in the south, and from the Adriatic coast in the west to the Black Sea in the east.

Unlike many previous conquerors, Philip did not destroy the cities and lands he invaded. He subdued their kings and royal families, but allowed the captured cities and tribes to govern themselves. He built new towns, improved agriculture, and increased the amount of money the lands could provide. Men from all parts of the empire were enlisted into his army and, thanks to his clever administration, Philip was able to pay them without demanding high taxes from his subjects.

Philip pursued a different policy with the Greek states from that which had brought him the rest of his empire. He tried diplomacy instead of conquest, and managed to win over most of Greece to his idea of a league of self-governing Greek states. Only Athens, Thebes, and a few others opposed him openly. When the two sides met in battle at Chaeronae in 338 B.C., the Macedonians were triumphant. As a result, all the Greek states apart from Sparta agreed to join forces with Macedonia against the great power of the Persian empire.

Philip's successes brought great power and prosperity to the Macedonians, and he was admired by many of his people. However, like all rulers, Philip also had enemies, he was assassinated in 336 B.C. This blow might have brought about the end of the Macedonian empire if it had not been for the extraordinary abilities of the man who succeeded Philip - his son, Alexander.

Alexander the Great

By acting quickly and intelligently, Alexander held the empire together. With a mixture of diplomacy and armed force, he put down rebellions in Greece, and in 334 B.C. he turned his attention to the Persians. Crossing from Europe to Asia, he defeated them in three great battles, the last at Gaugamela in 331 B.C., and overthrew their empire. He then began recruiting Asians into his army, building it up to 170,000 men, and leading it further east, as far as India.

Alexander next planned to conquer Arabia and return to the Mediterranean. With this in mind, he trained some of his new Asian recruits to oversee

Left: The empire of Alexander the Great at the time of his death in 323 B.C.

Right: At its largest, Alexander's army contained 170,000 soldiers, many of whom came from conquered lands.

PHILIP OF MACEDON RULES 359-336 B.C. • ALEXANDER CONQUERS PERSIANS 331 B.C.

Above: Part of a mosaic showing Alexander the Great in battle.

their own lands. But, at the height of his power, the greatest conqueror in history died of a fever. He was just 32 years old. In his short reign, he had created a multiracial kingdom, in which people of all nationalities could succeed if they were talented enough. Perhaps his most memorable achievement in Asia was the creation of 70 new towns - often called Alexandria - with mixed populations of Macedonians, Greeks, and Asians.

After Alexander's death, the empire was split into a number of kingdoms ruled by kings who had been generals in the army. These new kings fought among themselves for control of the heart of the empire - Macedonia itself. Their squabbles went on without interruption until 279 B.C., when the Gauls of western Europe invaded. They were turned back and Macedonia continued, with occasional gains and losses of territory, for several decades. Then, in 200 B.C., it came up against the growing power of Rome. Years of sporadic warfare followed until the Romans seized all Macedonian lands in 148 B.C.

DEATH OF ALEXANDER THE GREAT 323 B.C. • ROMANS CAPTURE MACEDONIA 148 B.C.

THE ROMAN REPUBLIC

The first settlement at Rome was a small group of huts built on the Palatine hill during the ninth century B.C. In the seventh century, when central Italy was ruled by the Etruscans, Rome developed from a small village to an important city. As the Etruscans' power declined, that of Rome grew, and the Roman people drove the Etruscans out of their city in around 510 B.C. and established a republic.

Below: A scene in the Senate, Rome's governing body.

Right: Rome and its surroundings at the time of the republic.

BIRTH OF ROMAN REPUBLIC 510 B.C. • WAR WITH CARTHAGE 264 TO 241 AND 218 TO 201 B.C.

ROMAN GODS

Here are just a few of the Romans' many gods and goddesses. At the top are Juno, the goddess of women, and her husband Jupiter, the king of the gods. Below them are Mars, the god of war, and Mercury, the gods' messenger, and Venus, the goddess of love.

The major powers in the region at that time were Greece and Carthage. Greece was engaged in fighting back the invading Persian empire, while Carthage was more interested in its trading empire in the western Mediterranean than in what was happening in Italy. As a result, the Roman republic was able to grow in size and power without much interference from outside.

Conquest

After Rome defeated the neighboring Latins in battle in 496 B.C., the two sides agreed in a series of treaties to fight together against outsiders. However, Rome was still unable to hold back the Celts when they surged into central Italy in 386 B.C. The city was overpowered and, although the Celts were driven out, it was 50 years before Rome became dominant once more. The Romans strengthened their army in 434 B.C. and set out to conquer more land. By 264 B.C., the whole of Italy was under their control.

As the Romans began to expand still further, they came into conflict with Carthage. During the First Punic War (264 to 241 B.C.) Rome captured Sicily, and then went on to take Corsica and Sardinia. In the Second Punic War (218 to 201 B.C.), despite the bravery of Hannibal and his army (see pages 52-53), Spain was seized from Carthage.

The Republic then looked eastward for new territories. Macedonia, Syria, Cilicia, Cyprus, and Crete all fell under Roman domination by 58 B.C. In Africa, Cyrene and Carthage were defeated, while in Europe, Rome captured all of what is now France. By 44 B.C., the entire Mediterranean world was under Roman control.

Roman Society

When the Roman republic was first established it was ruled by a group of long-established families, known as the patricians, and the ordinary citizens, or plebeians, had very little power. The slaves, who were far below even the plebeians on the social scale, had no power at all. The wealthy patricians lived in great luxury, with their slaves to do the work for them, both in their houses in the city and at their villas and farms in the country. Outside Rome, some provincial governors forced their subjects to pay huge taxes.

Over the years, the plebeians managed to take away some of the patricians' rights, but this was not enough to prevent the civil war that broke out during the first century B.C. This was caused by two Roman generals who were both trying to seize more power. Then, in 73 B.C., a slave called Spartacus led a revolt of 90,000 other slaves. The final blow to the Roman republic came when Julius Caesar and Pompey, two of the most important army generals, fought each other for control of the government. In the end, Caesar triumphed, and in about 48 B.C. he became the sole ruler, or dictator, of Rome.

CAESAR SOLE RULER OF ROME c.48 B.C. • ROME CONTROLS MEDITERRANEAN BY 44 B.C.

59

THE ROMAN EMPIRE

Four years after he had gained control of Rome, Julius Caesar was murdered and the empire was plunged into civil war. Octavian, Caesar's adopted son, succeeded in leading his supporters to victory against Brutus and Cassius - two of Caesar's assassins - and then defeated his other rivals for power, Mark Antony and the Egyptian queen Cleopatra. In doing so, Octavian became the master of the empire, and brought it a period of stability that was to last for 250 years.

Imperial Power

In 27 B.C. Octavian became Rome's first emperor, and from then on he was known as Augustus. During his rule he set about changing the way in which the empire was run. He reduced the size of the army and stationed many of its soldiers on the frontiers; he gave most of the empire's population the right to govern themselves; and he enabled talented people from all parts of the empire to rise to some of the most important positions in the government.

Thanks to Augustus' reforms, the empire remained peaceful and was able to concentrate on expanding its borders. Around A.D. 117, under Trajan, the Empire reached its greatest extent, and included England and Wales, all of Europe south of the Rhine and Danube rivers, western Asia south of the Black Sea, Syria, Egypt, and north Africa. At that time it had a population of 50 to 60 million.

The empire's wealth came mainly from agriculture and trade. Food and other goods were traded throughout the Mediterranean and beyond - to Britain, northern Europe and as far east as India. Most trade went by sea because this was easier than transporting goods by land. The empire was crisscrossed by an impressive system of roads, but they were used mainly by people on official business and for the movement of soldiers.

Life in Imperial Rome

At the heart of the empire was the city of Rome itself, home to one million people. It was a city of open squares, called forums, and imposing buildings. There was the Circus Maximus where chariot racing and athletics contests were held, and the Colosseum where, on public holidays, 70,000 bloodthirsty spectators could watch men fighting each other to the death, or being killed by wild animals. After a

Below: A Roman soldier from about A.D. 100, and the equipment he had to carry.

JULIUS CAESAR MURDERED 44 B.C. • OCTAVIAN BECOMES EMPEROR AUGUSTUS 27 B.C.

morning's work, Roman men could spend the afternoon at one of the many public baths; women went in the morning when men were not allowed in, or visited baths that were built especially for them. There were also markets, stores, temples, tombs built for past emperors, and, of course, houses.

Wealthy Roman families lived in large comfortable houses consisting of a number of rooms built around a courtyard, or *atrium*. There would be a kitchen, dining room, storerooms, bedrooms, servants' rooms, and a special room where guests were entertained. Some houses had lavatories that led into drains below, and some even had a hypocaust, a system of central heating in the form of hot air that flowed underneath the stone floors. The cooking, cleaning, and other household duties were all carried out by slaves.

The houses of poor people were very different. Most Romans lived in blocks of flats called *insulae*; when there was a shortage of housing, more flats were built on top of the blocks. Because of the risk of fire, people were not allowed to have stoves for cooking above the ground floor. There were plenty of carry-out stores where food could be bought and either eaten at once or taken home.

Above: The Roman empire at the time of Emperor Trajan in about A.D. 117.

Below: This large town house would have belonged to a wealthy Roman citizen.

ROMAN EMPIRE AT ITS LARGEST C.A.D. 117 • POPULATION 50 TO 60 MILLION

ROME'S DIVIDED EMPIRE

The expansion of the Roman Empire came to a halt during the rule of the emperor Trajan (A.D. 98-117). He gained control of Arabia and conquered Dacia, to the west of the Black Sea, and brought the empire to its greatest extent. To protect some of the empire's borders, fortified walls were built beyond the Rhine and Danube rivers, in Syria, and in north Africa. The most famous of these fortifications is Hadrian's Wall, in northern England, commissioned by and named after Trajan's successor.

Decline in the West

The following 100 years brought mixed fortunes. There were periods of war and peace, conspiracies in the Senate (the governing body), and assassinations of emperors. The murder of the emperor Alexander Severus in A.D. 235 marked the end of what we now regard as the golden age of Rome.

By the time Diocletian became emperor in A.D. 284, the empire had suffered countless invasions and had been ruled by 20 emperors. Another threat to the power of Rome was the spread of Christianity. Despite the repeated persecution of Christians - including feeding them to the lions in the Colosseum - Rome's emperors found it impossible to destroy the Church. Eventually, Christians were allowed to worship in peace, and the emperor Constantine (A.D. 307-337) even converted to Christianity, which gradually spread through much of the empire.

In the years before and during Constantine's rule, an important change had taken place in the empire. The center of power had shifted eastward and in A.D. 285 the empire had been divided into two halves for the purpose of administration. In A.D. 330, a new capital of the eastern empire had been established at Byzantium, which was renamed Constantinople, and is now Istanbul, the Turkish capital.

Nonetheless, in 337 the empire was still strong and capable of defending itself. Within a short time, however, the Romans came under concerted and constant attack from numerous "barbarians" outside

Below: A patrol of Roman soldiers leaving a fort along Hadrian's Wall.

EMPIRE DIVIDED A.D. 285 • CHRISTIANITY GROWS UNDER CONSTANTINE A.D. 307-337 the empire - the Picts, Scots, and Saxons in Britain; the Franks in Gaul; the Vandals in Spain; and the Visigoths, Ostrogoths, and Huns in eastern Europe and the Balkans. If they had all come separately, the Romans could probably have fought off these attacks, but almost the entire western half of the empire was affected and the pressure was enormous. Furthermore, the empire had been decaying on the inside for many years, as prices had risen constantly, conflict had grown between cities and the country people, and regional army commanders had fought among themselves for power.

Faced with the barbarian attacks, the Romans pulled back further and further, while attempting to make peace with the invaders. But these efforts failed: in A.D. 410 and 455, the city of Rome was overrun by the Visigoths and the Vandals. Finally, in 495, the Ostrogoths captured the whole of Italy and established it as their kingdom. The western part of Rome's once-great empire had crumbled.

Below: Emperor Constantine (right).

Right: Turks capturing Constantinople.

The Eastern Empire

The eastern half of the empire also came under attack, especially from the Huns, but it managed to weather the storm. For 200 years people carried on a Roman way of life, but gradually Greek replaced Latin as the official language and new systems of law were introduced. The so-called Byzantine empire that emerged survived for another 800 years until Constantinople was captured by the Turks in 1453.

WESTERN EMPIRE ATTACKED BY BARBARIANS c.370-495 • BYZANTINE EMPIRE 330-1453

JAPAN AND KOREA

Until about 1500 B.C., the people of Korea and Japan lived mainly by fishing, gathering plants from the wild, and growing vegetables. One of the major changes to their way of life came when rice and millet were introduced, first to Korea and then to western Japan about 1,000 years later.

Korea

These crops were brought to Korea from China. At first, the people of northern Korea grew mainly millet and soyabeans, while those in the south cultivated rice, but later on rice growing spread throughout the country.

The art of making bronze ornaments and weapons was also introduced to Korea from Manchuria, to the north of China, in around 1000 B.C. Early Korean bronze mirrors and daggers are very like those that were made in Manchuria, but gradually Korean craftsmen developed styles of their own. Only the wealthiest people could afford bronze, and from the objects found in Korean tombs it seems that most of these rich people lived in the south of the country; very few northern tombs contain bronzes. Bronze was not used to make everyday items: farmers continued to use tools which were made from stone and wood.

The Han dynasty of China took control of Korea in 108 B.C., but as they fell into decline from around A.D. 200, they were replaced by new groups. The first major civilizations that grew up in Korea were called the Shilla, Paekche, and Koguryo. The strongest of these was the Shilla, which spread outward from its base in the southeast and, by A.D. 668, had managed to unite the entire country.

Japan

The early people of Japan, known as the Jomon, depended heavily on fishing. However, when rice growing first appeared on the western island of Kyushu in around 500 B.C., a new culture developed, called the Yayoi. Like their predecessors in Korea, Yayoi farmers used wooden hoes and spades, and stone knives for cutting the seed heads from the rice plants. When the rice had been harvested, it was stored in special granaries that were built on stilts to keep it off the ground and therefore dry and protected from rats and mice.

Below: The early states which grew up in Korea and Japan before A.D. 300.

RICE GROWING INTRODUCED TO KOREA c.1500 B.C. • RICE REACHES JAPAN c.500 B.C.

64

By A.D. 300 rice growing had spread throughout the whole of Japan, apart from the island of Hokkaido in the far north. Also at that time Japan's first powerful state - the Yamato - developed in central Honshu. Yamato rulers were buried in huge tombs shaped like keyholes. The largest tomb that has been found belonged to the emperor Nintoku, who died in about A.D. 475. It covers a huge area, 519 yds. by 219 yds. and is surrounded by three water-filled moats. Around it are smaller tombs built for nobles. Buddhism reached Japan from China in around A.D. 550, and temples were then built instead of tombs.

As the Yamato state became stronger and started to expand northward, it came into conflict with the local populations it tried to control. On Hokkaido, the local people built a large number of hill-forts to defend themselves. By A.D. 700, however, most of Japan was under Yamato control. In A.D. 710, the Yamato state gave way to a new, unified Japanese state with its capital at Nara.

Left: A Yayoi rice granary.

Below: Emperor Nintoku's keyhole tomb.

RISE OF YAMATO STATE c.A.D. 300 • **BUDDHISM REACHES JAPAN FROM CHINA** c.A.D. 550

THE MAURYAN EMPIRE

Above: The Buddha teaching his followers. Asoka became a Buddhist in about 260 B.C.

When India's first great civilization - in the Indus Valley - collapsed in about 1500 BC, the area around the valley of the Ganges River became the cultural center. By 1000 B.C. iron tools were being used to clear land and cultivate crops of rice and wheat there. In the area now called Pakistan, a number of small states had grown up by 600 B.C., mostly around large towns and cities. Further to the east, the land around the Ganges River was held by people known as the Nandas, who had their capital at Pataliputra (modern-day Patna).

The Rise of the Mauryans

Among the groups that were ruled over by the Nandas were the Mauryans, and, in around 320 B.C., Chandragupta, their young leader, managed to bring down the Nanda dynasty and seize the throne. He was also able to capture the northwest of the country, Nepal, and a large part of the Deccan, India's central plateau.

Apart from a few details we do not know very much about the early Mauryans. It seems that Pataliputra was a large, wealthy city, stretching about 8½ mi. along the banks of the Ganges. It was protected by a strong timber rampart. Along the valley there was a shortage of hard stone and so the

buildings at Pataliputra, including Chandragupta's palace, were mostly wooden. It is said that Chandragupta was a strong, fair ruler, but that he lived in constant fear of being assassinated and slept in a different bedroom of his palace every night.

When Chandragupta had been king for 24 years, a great famine swept through his empire. He believed that it was because of his failure as a ruler, and gave up the throne. His lands were inherited by his son Bindusara, during whose reign the empire became steadily richer as more and more land was cultivated and trade increased.

Asoka and Buddhism

Bindusara died in about 270 B.C. and, after some fierce battles, his son Asoka became king. At first Asoka seems to have been a very harsh ruler; in 262 B.C. he put down a rebellion, in what is now Orissa, with enormous bloodshed. But he appears to have had a sudden change of heart.

This was as a result of his conversion from Hinduism to Buddhism, a religion which had begun

MAURYANS RISE UNDER CHANDRAGUPTA c.320-296 B.C. • ASOKA BECOMES KING 270 B.C.

about 250 years earlier. Its founder, the Buddha or "enlightened one," had preached against greed and war, and told people that if they acted wisely their lives would be happier. Asoka obeyed the words of the Buddha and dramatically changed the way in which he ruled. He devised a moral code based on Buddhist teachings, instructing people on how to behave. The code was carved on rock faces and specially constructed pillars throughout the empire. Beyond the borders of his empire, the conquest of foreign lands was stopped.

However, Asoka's conversion had a rather drastic effect on the Mauryan empire. In his later life, Asoka spent more time talking with Buddhist monks than he did on overseeing the administration. By the time of his death in 232 B.C., the empire had already begun to crumble. After a palace revolt in about 186 B.C., the Mauryans were replaced by a new Hindu dynasty, the Sungas.

Right: This lion carving was a symbol of Asoka's authority and goodness.

Below: Many stupas, or Buddhist sacred mounds, were built during Asoka's reign.

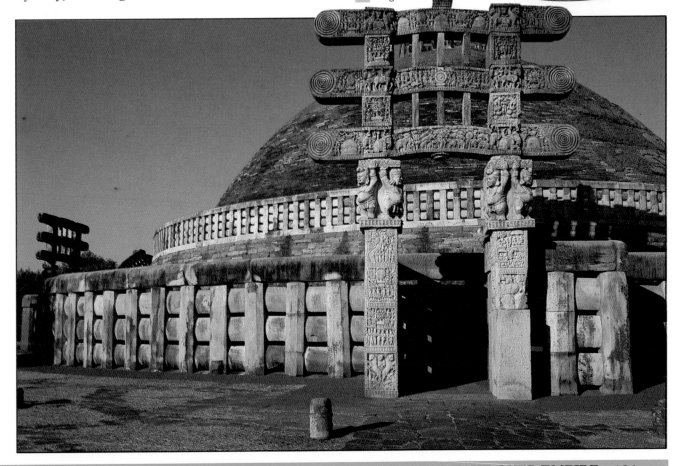

ASOKA'S CONVERSION TO BUDDHISM c.260 B.C. • SUNGAS TAKE OVER EMPIRE c.186 B.C.

AFTER ALEXANDER

Above: The city of Ctesiphon, beside the Euphrates River, became the Parthian capital in the first century B.C. and was taken over by the Sassanians 400 years later.

Left: When the Seleucid empire was broken up after 192 B.C., part of it was taken over by the Parthians. Their empire fell to the Sassanians in A.D. 226.

Right: This silver-gilt dish shows King Ardashir III, who ruled from A.D. 628 to 630, near the end of the Sassanian empire. Hunting was a favorite royal pastime.

SELEUCID EMPIRE RULES PERSIA 312-192 B.C. • PARTHIAN EMPIRE 171 B.C.-A.D. 226

Following the death of Alexander the Great, the Persian part of the Macedonian empire was taken over by Seleucus in 312 B.C. Almost immediately he was faced with rebellions and attacks from outside his empire. Early in his reign he was forced to give up the area around the Indus River to the increasingly powerful Mauryans, and under later Seleucid rulers, Syria and other lands were lost. Finally, in 192 B.C., the armies of republican Rome crushed the Seleucids and the empire broke up into a number of independent kingdoms and provinces.

The Parthians

Among these kingdoms was Parthia, a land to the southeast of the Caspian Sea. From 171 B.C. it was ruled by Mithridates, who conquered Babylonia and transformed the Parthians into the major power in the region.

The Parthians were, however, surrounded by enemies. When Mithridates II extended his empire westward to the Euphrates River, he came up against the Romans; in the east, attacks by the Kushans and Scythians kept Parthian troops on the defensive. There was also rebellion within the empire itself. Through frequent intrigues and murders, a succession of rulers took the Parthian throne. This weak-

ened the empire and gave Rome an excuse to intervene. At first, the Romans simply supported one or another of the rival claimants to the Parthian throne. But finally, the Roman emperor Trajan invaded Parthia.

The Romans' influence was short lived, but Parthia was soon threatened from other directions and the empire steadily shrank in size. Eventually, the Sassanian kingdom of Iran broke what little power the Parthians had.

The Sassanian Empire

Under the Sassanian king Ardashir a new kingdom of Iran was founded after the defeat of the Parthians in A.D. 226. His son, Shapur I, expanded the kingdom to include all of modern Iran and parts of what are now Afghanistan, Pakistan, the U.S.S.R., Iraq, and the Persian Gulf coast. As had happened before, the growing empire attracted the attention of the Romans, who tried and failed to defeat the Sassanians in A.D. 244.

A few years later, Shapur decided to go on the offensive and he conquered Syria. Again the Romans attacked, launching a disastrous assault in which their emperor, Valerian, was captured. In the east, Shapur added the territory of the Kushans to his growing empire.

Shapur died in A.D. 276, and during the 30 years that followed, his successors lost nearly all of the lands he had gained. But out of the chaos there emerged a new leader, Shapur II, who became one of the strongest rulers in Sassanian history. He recovered the lost territories and, after brief skirmishes with the Romans, captured the province of Armenia.

Following the death of Shapur II in A.D. 339, two new threats faced the Sassanian empire. One of these was the nobles within the empire, who were becoming increasingly powerful. The other came from nomadic tribes, called the Hepthalites, beyond the northeastern border. In A.D. 484, the Sassanian King Peroz was killed in battle and from then on the Sassanians were dominated by the Hepthalites. They recovered some of their former glory under Khusrao I (A.D. 531-579), but between 633 and 642 the empire was conquered by the Arabs - followers of the Muslim prophet Muhammad.

RISE OF SASSANIAN EMPIRE A.D. 226-276 • ARABS CONQUER SASSANIANS A.D. 633-642

HAN CHINA

For almost 200 years, from 403 to 221 B.C., China was torn by constant war among seven of its major states. Gradually one state, Ch'in, became the most powerful of the seven and established control over the whole of China. In 221 B.C., King Chen of Ch'in took the title of Shih Huang-ti, or First Emperor of China. When he died, thousands of life-size terra-cotta soldiers and horses were made and placed in Shih Huang-ti's tomb to guard him.

The rule of the Ch'in dynasty was very harsh and people who opposed it were punished ruthlessly. Eventually, rebellions broke out in several regions and in 206 B.C. the empire collapsed into civil war.

Conquest and Trade

In 202 B.C. a new dynasty, the Han, gained control. During the first 70 years of their rule, the Han strengthened their hold on China. The country was divided into a number of kingdoms and command-eries that were responsible to the emperor and the government in Chang'an, the capital. By about 135 B.C. the Han had established firm control over the whole country and began to look beyond their borders. They invaded and captured territories in the north-east, south, and southwest. Han armies also attacked the nomadic Hsiung-nu tribes to the north but were unable to defeat them totally. In earlier times, some northern Chinese kingdoms had built defensive walls and manned them with soldiers to keep out the Hsiung-nu. The Ch'in emperors had rebuilt and strengthened these defences to create the Great Wall, and the Han emperor Wu-ti further extended the Wall to the northwest. Protected

Below left: By 135 B.C. the Han dynasty had gained control of the country.

Below: Under the Han dynasty, trade flourished and China became very wealthy.

KOREA

JAPAN

●LUOYANG

CHANG'AN

RIVER YANGTZE CHINA

INDIA

HAN EMPIRE
GREAT WALL OF CHINA

SHIH HUANG-TI FIRST CHINESE EMPEROR 221 B.C. • START OF HAN DYNASTY 202 B.C.

TERRACOTTA WARRIORS

When Shih Huang-ti, the first Chinese emperor, died he was buried in a tomb guarded by an army of more than 7,000 life-size pottery figures, including footsoldiers, bowmen and spearmen, and horses and chariots. The faces of the warriors are all different, and they may have been modeled on real people. The tomb was buried under a huge earth mound, and it probably took 700,000 laborers about 36 years to build. It was found in 1974 by farmers who were digging a well for water near the village of Xian.

behind the Great Wall, the Han conquered lands to the west and began a very profitable silk trade both with the Parthian empire in Persia and with the Roman empire.

The silk trade made the Han very wealthy. The richest people had a very luxurious way of life, as can be seen from the artifacts that were buried with them when they died. Beautiful objects made of gold, bronze, jade, silk, lacquer, and pottery have been found in Han tombs, along with many everyday items, such as clothes, food, and musical instruments. People believed that all these things would be needed in the afterlife.

Ironworking was a very important industry in Han China, and there were 49 huge foundries throughout the country, producing household objects and agricultural tools such as plowshares. In order to feed the population of 57 million people, farmers grew millet, rice, and Chinese cabbages, and raised pigs, dogs, and chickens for food. Other types of food were imported from India and further afield.

The Hsin Dynasty

From around 90 B.C. the Han empire began to weaken. The military campaigns that were launched to capture more territory cost a huge amount of money and were not always successful. Following the death of Wu-ti, a succession of weak emperors came to the throne, and the authority of the Han was challenged. In A.D. 9, Wang Mang seized the throne and set up the Hsin dynasty. His reign was ended in A.D. 23 by widespread rebellions and the Han returned to power.

During the first century AD trade flourished again and landowners, merchants, and the upper classes became very rich. In about 100 A.D., the art of paper making was invented in China. Soft tree fibers were mashed in water, pressed flat and finally dried to make paper.

From the middle of the second century, the empire was weakened by power struggles in the capital and uprisings in the countryside. Although the Han continued to rule for some years, power was really in the hands of a number of regional warlords. When the last Han emperor gave up the throne in A.D. 220, the empire was broken up into three separate states and China was not reunited until A.D. 589.

CHINA RULED BY HSIN DYNASTY A.D. 9-23 • HAN DYNASTY BACK IN POWER A.D. 23-220

THE KUSHANS

Left: The Kushan empire reached its largest extent after A.D. 78, under King Kaniska.

TAXILA

RIVER INDUS

RIVER GANGES

BARBARICUM

VARANASI

BARYGAZA

KUSHAN EMPIRE

Below: Silk from China passed through the Kushan city of Taxila on its journey west.

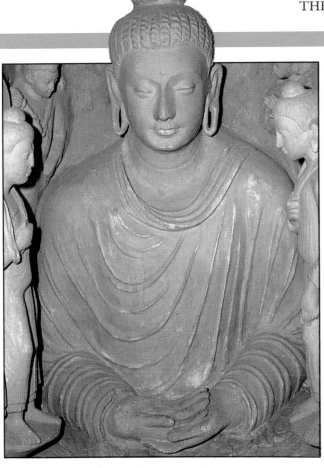

Above: A statue from Taxila of the Buddha, carved in the Gandharan style.

The history of the Kushan empire of India has its beginnings in China. When Shih Huang-ti, China's first emperor, united his country in 221 B.C., the nomadic tribes who lived in the pasturelands on the western borders were driven out. These tribes, the Hsiung-nu and Yueh-chih, were forced to move into central Asia.

The Yueh-chih settled in the valley of the Oxus in River about 165 B.C. They did not immediately spread into India, mainly because they were not a united tribe but were split into five separate groups. Eventually one of these groups, the Kushans, defeated the other four and began a period of conquest.

The Kushans in India

Kadphises I, the first Kushan ruler, extended his territories to the Indus Valley. He was succeeded by Kadphises II, who conquered most of the area known as the Punjab. Kaniska, the third and most powerful king, Kaniska, came to the throne in about A.D. 78. During his reign he gained control of an empire that stretched from Varanasi in the Ganges River valley to deep inside central Asia.

Within the empire there was a wide range of different cultures, including Indian, Chinese, central Asian, Greek, and Roman. This was reflected in the art which was produced; for example, the sculptures of Gandhara in northwest India are a mixture of Indian and Greek styles.

India had trade links with the Middle East and Egypt dating from centuries earlier. During the time of the Kushan empire, and especially under Kaniska, these links were strengthened and new ones added. By the first century A.D. the Roman historian Pliny recorded that Indian spices, jewels, textiles, and exotic animals were being imported by the Roman empire. Spice traders in the Kushan empire, eager to satisfy the demand of their customers overseas, traveled throughout Southeast Asia buying local spices. For a time, a great deal of the Chinese silk trade passed through the Indian city of Taxila on its way westward. Indian ports such as Barbaricum on the delta of the Indus River and Barygaza near the mouth of the Narmada River, were shipping cargoes of diamonds, turquoise, indigo, tortoise shells, and silks. In return copper, pearls, wine, gold, slaves, and dates were imported from the Mediterranean region, Arabia, and Ethiopia.

The Kushan empire was at its height when the Romans were at their most powerful. Because of the Kushans' position between east and west, aspects of Western culture passed through them into India and beyond. The Kushans also helped to spread the teachings of Buddhism throughout their empire and into China.

The Decline of the Kushans

After Kaniska died in about 100 A.D. the Kushans' power began to fade in the Ganges valley. In the third century A.D. they came up against the new Sassanian rulers of Persia, and other parts of their empire were taken by invading nomadic tribes. From this time onward, the Kushan dynasty never again played an important part in the affairs of Asia.

KANISKA DIES c.100 A.D. • KUSHAN EMPIRE FADES IN THIRD CENTURY A.D.

NORTH AMERICA

For thousands of years after the first settlers reached North America from Siberia, hunting and gathering was the main way in which people lived. There was a vast range of animals to be hunted for food, including deer, elks, mountain sheep, and ducks. Rabbits were trapped or snared, and fish were caught in rivers. Many plants could also be gathered.

The Basketmakers

There were hundreds of different groups of hunter-gatherers living in North America before the first century A.D. The people living in the southwest are now known as Basketmakers, because archaeologists have found many examples of the wicker baskets that they used for gathering food. Between A.D. 1 and 500, crop growing seems to have become more important, as people began to live in small clusters of huts overlooking areas of fertile land where they grew corn. Most food, however, was still gathered from the wild.

After A.D. 500 river flood plains were cultivated and crops of corn, beans, and other plants were grown. The villages in which people lived became larger, with up to 50 houses surrounded by grain storage pits. The houses were partly dug into the ground, and the walls inside were lined with stone slabs covered with thick plaster. The bow and arrow was first introduced during this period, replacing the spear as the weapon used for hunting. Pottery making also began at this time - a useful skill that was passed on from a neighboring group called the Mogollon.

The Hopewell

In eastern North America, in the woodlands to the west of the Appalachian Mountains, other cultures were flourishing. Among them were the Hopewell people, who lived in a vast area south of the Great Lakes from about 300 B.C. They were mainly hunter- gatherers, living off the abundant resources

Below: Basketmaker houses were built partly underground and were entered through the roof.

Right: Lands occupied by the Basketmaker and Hopewell peoples of North America.

FIRST CULTIVATION OF CORN C.A.D. 1-500 • GREAT SERPENT MOUND BUILT A.D. 200

Above: The Great Serpent Mound is a massive earthwork built for religious ceremonies.

in the wild, but they also grew crops of corn. Because hunting and gathering were very important, villages were built close to areas rich in edible plants and game, rather than near the most fertile agricultural land.

Hopewell artists carved beautiful shapes in wood, stone, and bone. They often obtained their raw materials from far away: shells, shark teeth, and turtle shells were brought from Florida; grizzly bear teeth and obsidian came from the Rocky Mountains, and copper and silver were traded from around the Great Lakes.

The Hopewell people built huge mounds and other earthworks, probably for religious ceremonies. One of the most spectacular is the Great Serpent Mound in Ohio, which is 712 ft. long and in the shape of a huge snake. It was built in A.D. 200. The fact that these earthworks must have needed an enormous number of people to build them shows

that there was no shortage of food. Dead chieftains were buried in the mounds, along with tools, pottery, bowls, jewelry, and other items that it was believed would be needed in the afterlife.

The first real towns in North America did not appear until about A.D. 700, in the valley of the Mississippi River. They were built around flat-topped mounds on which temples were constructed. A typical town had about 20 of these mounds inside a wooden stockade for protection. One of the largest of these towns was Cahokia, which had a population of about 10,000 people and contained more than 100 temple mounds.

In the sixteenth century, European explorers reached this part of North America and found the towns with their temple mounds. Tragically, the explorers brought diseases to which the native people had no resistance, and thousands of them died. Others were killed violently by the newcomers.

THE GUPTA EMPIRE

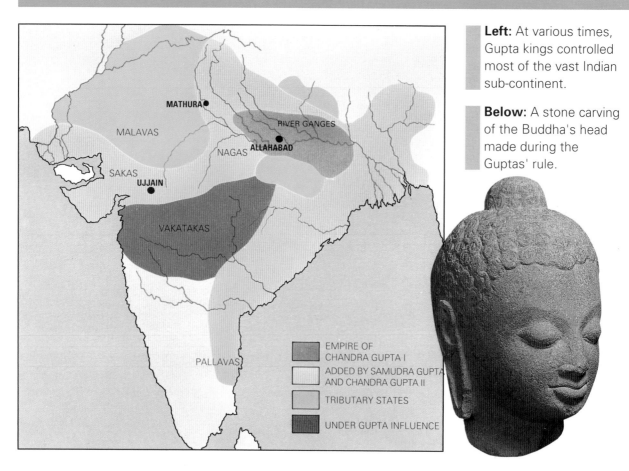

Left: At various times, Gupta kings controlled most of the vast Indian sub-continent.

Below: A stone carving of the Buddha's head made during the Guptas' rule.

EMPIRE OF CHANDRA GUPTA I
ADDED BY SAMUDRA GUPTA AND CHANDRA GUPTA II
TRIBUTARY STATES
UNDER GUPTA INFLUENCE

During the fourth century A.D. a new dynasty appeared in the Ganges valley of India, in the area known as Magadha. At first the Gupta kingdom was simply one among many in the region, but in A.D. 320 Chandra Gupta I its new ruler, began to expand his power. During his 15-year reign he gained control over the whole Ganges valley, from Allahabad in the west to the borders of Bengal in the east.

A Growing Empire

When Chandra Gupta died in 335, his son Samudra Gupta came to the throne. He used the empire which his father had created as a base from which to conquer more territory. He led an expedition into south India and reached Kanchi, the capital of a dynasty called the Pallavas. On the way he subdued many smaller kingdoms and forced them to pay him tribute (money or valuable goods) to show their allegiance to him. The wealth he gained in this way was used to pay for other campaigns in the north of

India. He was so successful that by the time of his death in A.D. 376, only one other independent kingdom of any size remained in the northern part of India - that of the Sakas.

Samudra was followed by Chandra Gupta II, his son, who became the most powerful of all Gupta rulers. He went a step further than his father and conquered the Sakas; he may also have used their capital, Ujjain, as his own headquarters. By marrying a member of the Vakataka dynasty in central India, he also became the overlord of that kingdom, although only for a short time.

It has been said that during Chandra Gupta II's reign India was the most civilized country in the world; in the west the Roman empire was under attack from the barbarians, and China was also in crisis. Chandra Gupta II was certainly a highly civilized ruler, and his name is linked with the finest writers of the time, such as the poet Kalidasa.

EXPANSION OF GUPTA EMPIRE A.D. 320-414 • PEACE UNDER KUMARA GUPTA A.D. 414-454

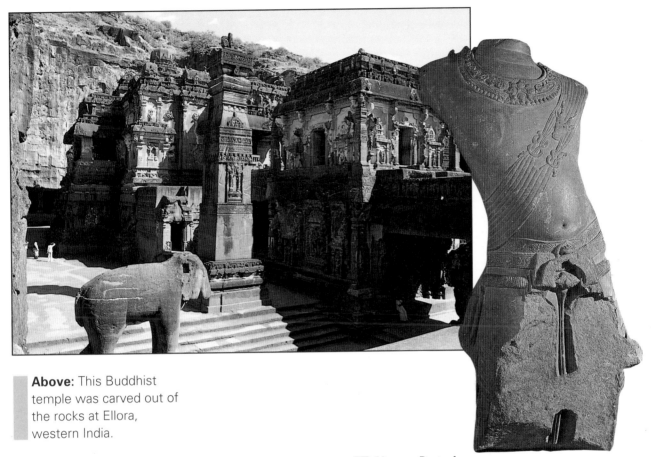

The Hepthalites

The empire continued to thrive under its next ruler, Kumara Gupta. During most of his reign, from A.D. 414 to 454, northern India was peaceful and prosperous, and the arts continued to flourish; some of the finest Indian painting to have survived was done during this time.

Toward the end of Kumara's rule, after a period of expansion which had lasted more than 100 years, the fortunes of the Guptas began to change. A nomadic group called the Hepthalites, or White Huns, had seized parts of central Asia and Afghanistan in the fourth century, and in the middle of the fifth century they captured most of the Punjab. In around A.D. 450, the Guptas came under direct attack and their power was shaken. Kumara died during this war and his place was taken by his son, Skanda Gupta. The new ruler managed to fight off the Hepthalites, but soon afterward other threats appeared.

Above: Part of a fifth-century Bodhisattva (divine being) carved in the Gupta style.

Beyond the Ganges plain - the heartland of the Gupta empire - provincial governors were beginning to set themselves up as kings, ignoring the power of the Gupta rulers. Gradually the empire shrank to the size it had been under Chandra Gupta I. Furthermore, the Hepthalites once again turned their attentions toward India, and in 500 they attacked in force. Although they were eventually pushed back to Kashmir in the northwest, the Hepthalites damaged the Guptas' power beyond repair. Countless new kingdoms sprang up, taking advantage of the Guptas' weakness. The empire survived in some parts of northeast India until about A.D. 650, but it was an empire in name only.

FIRST ATTACKS BY HEPTHALITES c.A.D. 450 • GUPTA EMPIRE GROWS WEAKER FROM c.475

INDEX

ACKNOWLEDGEMENTS

The publishers would like to thank the following organizations and individuals for their kind permission to reproduce the pictures in this book:

Ancient Art & Architecture/R. Sheridan 9, 19, 30, 43, 77; Michael Holford 10, 12, 17, 24, 35, 40, 54, 66, 76, 77; Robert Harding Picture Library 11, 15, 23, 36-37, 41, 46, 47, 48, 51, 67, 68 front cover centre; C. M. Dixon 15, 21, 26, 27, 30, 33, 57, 63, 69; Cambridge University Library 16; Sonia Halliday 28, 35, 46, 53; Werner Forman 36; Aerofilms 39; Mansell Collection 63; Magnum/I. Morath 71; Peter Newark Pictures 75; Douglas Dickins 73; Georg Gerster 65; Hutchison Library front cover left.
Illustrations by:

Richard Berridge (Specs Art Agency) - pages 12 - 13, 14-15, 19, 26 - 27, 30 - 31, 52 - 53, 54 - 55, 57, 59, 70 - 71, 72
Wayne Ford - page 7
Finbarr O'Connor - pages 11, 16, 20 - 21, 23 right, 24-25, 29, 38 - 39, 42, 44, 60, 62
The Maltings Partnership - pages 8, 22 - 23, 33, 61, 74
Mark Stacey - pages 6, 7, 34 - 35, 45, 49, 58, 64 -65, pull-out time chart

Illustrations in top right-hand corners by Joe Lawrence

All maps plus page 24 inset by Peter Bull Art Studios

The illustrations in the top right-hand corners of the right hand pages in this book show the following:
Page 7, Altimira cave painting; page 9, wheat and barley; page 11, 'Ram in Thicket' from Sumer; page 13, Egyptian wall painting; page 15, statue of a god or priest-king from Mohenjo-Daro; page 17, Shang jade spearhead; page 19, statue of Anubis from Tutankhamun's tomb; page 21, stag shield centerpiece from Scythian tomb; page 23, early navigation chart; page 25, Minoan double-headed axe; page 27, bull's head from Babylon, page 29, Hittite chariot; page 31, lion gate at Mycenae; page 33, Phoenician bust; page 35, the Ark of the Covenant; page 37, Olmec stone head; page 39 Celtic brooch; page 41, Etruscan terracotta head of warrior; page 43, Assyrian siege machine; page 45, Greek vase; page 47, funerary statuette from Qataban; page 49, Nok head; page 51, Persian gold armlet from Oxus treasure; page 53, statuette of Carthaginian warrior; page 55, bronze voting disks; page 57, cameo of Alexander the Great and his wife Roxanne; page 59, she-wolf symbolising Rome's greatness; page 61, SPQR symbol of Rome; page 63, head of Constantine the Great; page 65, statuette of Japanese warrior; page 67, the Buddhist Stupa at Sanchi; page 69, Sassanian relief; page 71, Chinese lacquer bowl; page 73, Kushan statue of a tree spirit; page 75, North American decoy duck from Nevada; page 77, Chandra Gupta I and his queen on gold coin

Illustrations in the pull-out time chart show, from left to right:

Neanderthal man; a Shang bronze artefact (top); a Hittite statue; the Hanging Gardens of Babylon; a Macedonian spearman; a rock tomb at Petra; Chinese paper making; a Greek discus thrower; ancient Rome; Olmec head (top); South American crop growing; a Mayan; Spaniards arriving in Central America

TIME CHART

Only approximate dates can be given for the earliest events.

B.C.

4 million	First Hominids in Africa
2.5 million	Stone tools first used
1.7 million	First hunters
200,000	Neanderthals in Africa
100,000	First modern humans in Africa
8000	Earliest pottery in Sahara
7500	First farmers in Fertile Crescent
7000	Çatal Hüyük founded and first farming in Indus valley
6500	Earliest known textiles
5500	First irrigation in Mesopotamia
4000	Bronze first introduced
3500	First cities and rise of Sumer

3300	First Egyptian cities
3100	Earliest written language in Sumer and unification of Egypt
3000	Egyptian hieroglyphics
2700	Bronze made in China and start of Old Kingdom in Egypt
2500	Rise of Indus Valley civilization and first bronze in South East Asia
2450	Great Pyramid of Khufu
2150	Collapse of Old Kingdom
2040	Middle Kingdom starts
2000	Earliest use of iron
1800	Two-wheeled war chariot and start of Chinese Shang dynasty
1783	End of Middle Kingdom in Egypt
1760	Rise of Babylon
1650	Rise of Hittites
1570	Egypt's New Kingdom starts

1500	Collapse of Indus civilization
1400	First Chinese writing
1200	Collapse of Hittite empire and Moses leads Hebrews out of Egypt
1166	Death of Pharaoh Rameses III
1085	Fall of New Kingdom
1027	End of Shang dynasty in China
1000	Phoenician trading empire at its height
950	Foundation of Assyrian empire
900	Start of kingdom of Kush
800	City states in Ganges Valley
750	Phoenicians settle Carthage
700	Assyrians capture Phoenician cities and first permanent Scythian Steppe settlements
650	First use of coins in west Asia
625	Babylon rises again
612	Fall of Assyrian empire
600	Hanging Gardens of Babylon

563	Birth of Siddhartha Gautama (the Buddha)	**312**	Start of Seleucid empire	**A.D.**	
559	Foundation of Achaemenids empire in Persia	**221**	China unified under first emperor, Shih Huangti	**60**	Rise of Kushan empire in India
550	First ironworking in China and rise of Red Sea states	**202**	Han dynasty starts in China	**105**	Paper used in China
539	Babylon falls to Persians	**186**	End of Mauryan empire	**220**	Collapse of Han dynasty
500	Rice grown in Japan	**171**	Parthian empire under Mithridates	**226**	Sassanians conquer Parthian empire
450	First iron in sub-Saharan Africa	**146**	Romans destroy Carthage	**300**	Decline of Red Sea states
403	Start of Chinese Warring States period	**108**	Han dynasty controls Korea	**304**	Hsiungnu nomads invade China
400	Rise of Carthage	**100**	Nabataean city of Petra at its height and camel introduced in Sahara	**320**	Foundation of Gupta empire in India
330	Fall of Persian empire			**400**	First towns in sub-Saharan Africa
329	Empire of Alexander the Great at its height			**475**	Tomb of emperor Nintoku in Japan
320	Chandragupta founds Mauryan empire in India			**480**	Fall of Gupta empire
				500	Bantu speakers arrive in southern Africa
				622	Rise of Islam under Muhammad
				641	Arabs conquer Egypt and spread into North Africa
				642	Sassanian empire falls to Arabs

B.C.

850,000 Hominids in Europe

35,000 Modern humans

6500 Crop and livestock farming begins

4200 World's first copper mines

3200 Wheeled vehicles in Europe

2000 Rise of Minoans on Crete and completion of Stonehenge in Britain

1900 Hieroglyphic writing reaches Crete

1650 Linear A script in Crete

1550 Beginning of Mycenaean Greece

1450 Collapse of Minoan Crete

1200 First Phoenician colonies in Mediterranean

1150 Collapse of Mycenaeans

850 First settlement at Rome

800 Start of iron age in Europe, spread of Celtic culture, rise of Etruscans, and rise of Greek city-states

776 Olympic Games first held in Greece

750 First Greek colonies around Mediterranean

700 Start of Archaic Greece

690 Etruscan writing developed

600 Rome becomes a city and first Greek coins made

509 Start of Roman republic

500 Carthage becomes independent state

480 Rise of classical civilization in Greece

462 Parthenon built in Athens

450 Athens at its peak

431 Start of Peloponnesian War between Athens and Sparta

390 Celts attack Rome

359 Philip becomes king of Macedonia

323 Death of Alexander the Great

300 First Celtic coins

264 Rome controls all of Italy

218 Hannibal leads Carthaginian army across Alps to attack Rome

206 Roman empire takes Spain

148 Romans capture Macedonia

146 Carthage destroyed by Romans

100 First large fortified settlements built by Celts

48 Julius Caesar becomes sole ruler of Rome

44 Caesar assassinated

27 Augustus first Roman emperor

A.D.

43 Romans invade Britain

50 Rome is world's largest city, with 1 million people

100 Roman army at its height, with 100,000 soldiers

117 Roman empire at its greatest extent at death of emperor Trajan

125 Hadrian's Wall built in Britain by Romans

150 Celts conquered by Romans

285 Division of Roman empire into eastern and western halves

330 Emperor Constantine founds Constantinople as capital of eastern empire

410 Sack of Rome by Visigoths

495 Ostrogoths establish kingdom in Italy

610 Eastern Roman empire becomes Byzantine empire

1453 Turks conquer Byzantine empire

B.C.

50,000 First modern humans in Australia

40,000 Modern humans in North America

30,000 First settlements in South America

10,000 Settlements near southern tip of South America

8500 Cultivation of crops in Peru

7000 First crops grown in Central America

5000 Maize first grown

4000 Earliest pottery in the Americas

3500 Cotton grown in Peru

2500 Extensive trade network in South America

1500 First metalworking

1200 Rise of Olmec civilization in Central America and Lapita colonists arrive in Melanesia

1000 Lapita settlers on Tonga and Samoa

900 Start of Chavín civilization in Andes

800 First writing in the Americas

310 Rise of Hopewell people in North America

300 Beginning of Maya civilization and collapse of Olmecs

200 Polynesians settle Marquesas Islands

A.D.

1 Basketmaker people begin cultivating corn in North America

200 Great Serpent Mound built by Hopewell people

300 Maya civilization reaches peak and first Maya cities built

400 Polynesians colonize Hawaiian Islands

500 Basketmaker peoples begin cultivating fertile river flood plains

700 Temple mounds in Mississippi, and first town in North America at Cahokia

800 First use of bow and arrow for hunting

800 Polynesians reach Easter Island

850 Maya civilization begins to decline

900 Polynesians settle New Zealand

1300 Maya civilization rises again

1493 First Spanish settlement in the Americas

1500 European explorers in North America

1517 Spaniards arrive in Central America